Incility

The Guilford Practical Intervention in the Schools Series

Kenneth W. Merrell, Series Editor

Books in this series address the complex academic, behavioral, and social–emotional needs of children and youth at risk. School-based practitioners are provided with practical, research-based, and readily applicable tools to support students and team successfully with teachers, families, and administrators. Each volume is designed to be used directly and frequently in planning and delivering educational and mental health services. Features include lay-flat binding to facilitate photocopying, step-by-step instructions for assessment and intervention, and helpful, timesaving reproducibles.

Recent Volumes

Inclusive Assessment and Accountability

*A Guide to Accommodations
for Students with Diverse Needs*

SARA E. BOLT
ANDREW T. ROACH

Foreword by Rachel F. Quenemoen

THE GUILFORD PRESS
New York   London

© 2009 The Guilford Press
A Division of Guilford Publications, Inc.
72 Spring Street, New York, NY 10012
www.guilford.com

Printed in Canada

This book is printed on acid-free paper.

Last digit is print number: 9 8 7 6 5 4 3 2 1

Library of Congress Cataloging-in-Publication Data

Bolt, Sara E.
  Inclusive assessment and accountability: a guide to accommodations for students with diverse needs / Sara E. Bolt, Andrew T. Roach.
      p.   cm. — (The Guilford practical intervention in the schools series)
  Includes bibliographical references and index.
  ISBN 978-1-60623-019-0 (pbk: alk. paper)
  1. Children with disabilities—Education—United States.   2. Children with disabilities—Education—United States—Evaluation.   3. Special education—United States.   I. Roach, Andrew T.   II. Title.
  LC4031 .B65 2009
  371.9—dc22

                                                                              2008038824

To my parents, Martin and Nancy; brothers, Dan and Mike; and sister, Laura; all of you have been an important source of support for my work on this project
—S. E. B.

To my parents, Dave and Lois, and my sister, Jennifer, for their love and support
—A. T. R.

About the Authors

Sara E. Bolt, PhD, is Assistant Professor of School Psychology at Michigan State University in East Lansing. She has a doctorate in educational psychology from the University of Minnesota. While completing her graduate studies, she worked as a research assistant at the National Center on Educational Outcomes and as a school psychologist at Heartland Area Education Agency. Dr. Bolt currently conducts research on testing accommodations for students with disabilities as well as on educational assessment practices for special populations generally.

Andrew T. Roach, PhD, is Assistant Professor in the Department of Counseling and Psychological Services at Georgia State University in Atlanta. His research focuses on alternate assessments and the alignment between standards, assessments, and classroom instruction. Dr. Roach received the 2007 Early Career Publication Award from the Council for Exceptional Children—Division of Research for an article on the effects of curricular access on students' alternate assessment performance. He has conducted alignment and related validity studies for alternate assessments in Georgia, Idaho, Indiana, Mississippi, and Wisconsin, and currently serves as coinvestigator on two federally funded investigations of the validity of alternate assessments based on modified achievement standards. Before completing his doctorate, Dr. Roach taught elementary and middle school for 9 years.

Foreword

Inclusive Assessment and Accountability: A Guide to Accommodations for Students with Diverse Needs is an important contribution to the tools available for educators at all levels of the public school system in the United States. Sara E. Bolt and Andrew T. Roach share not only their academic expertise but also their experience working directly with state and local educators on policy and practice issues related to large-scale assessment for system accountability. Their grounding in the field and understanding of current state and local practice make this book a practical and powerful resource.

Drs. Bolt and Roach caution that this is a "point-in-time" analysis, and it is important for readers to understand that caution. The policies and mandates that surround testing for accountability and define the purpose and uses of testing programs have everything to do with the options available to practitioners. In that context, the authors have provided resources that do change with the times—such as links to many dynamic Web-based tools—that the reader can tap. By incorporating multiple and varied resources such as extant research citations and practical tools for immediate use, along with resources that will evolve with the advent of new policies, research findings, and practice discoveries, they invite the reader to learn with them into the future and to join their virtual community of practice around the important topic of inclusive assessment.

A foundational assumption in the use of these marvelous resources is that the large-scale tests the authors discuss are designed for the purpose of *system* accountability. Making decisions about how students show us what they know on an assessment requires a clear understanding of the intended purpose(s) for which the test was designed and the intended use(s) of test results. When a test is designed to demonstrate how well students are being taught the challenging content for their enrolled grade level, we have different rules for how they participate than when we make decisions about participation in a test designed to demonstrate specific individual skills and knowledge for diagnostic purposes. A criterion-referenced test that appropriately measures content and achievement standards for a given grade and content area and is otherwise accessible for students with varying disabilities or language differences may indeed be "too hard" for a student who has not been taught that content. Such a result—showing that the student did not perform well on the content he or she had not been taught—is a valid inference for the purpose of system accountability.

That is probably the most common misunderstanding about testing for system account-ability, a misunderstanding that gets in the way of good local implementation of state tests. The mistaken zeal to have one test meet multiple (and sometimes contradictory) purposes and uses among policymakers and practitioners has muddied the waters of appropriate use across the country. A push for basic assessment literacy must have this approach as a founda-tion—one large-scale assessment cannot and should not meet all needs for educational data. The letter and the spirit of the No Child Left Behind Act of 2001 and the reauthorization of the Individuals with Disabilities Education Act of 2004 share a focus on a standards-based reform agenda: that states can set challenging content and achievement standards that are targets for learning for all students, and that schools then design the instruction and cur-riculum that will ensure all students can achieve to these expectations, with the bookend of statewide system accountability through large-scale assessment and accountability pro-grams. The assessments that Drs. Bolt and Roach cover in this book are those designed as part of this standards-based reform agenda.

The point the authors make—that knowledge is power—means that varied state and local choices can be implemented within the letter and spirit of the federal education laws, but they require informed stakeholder involvement and commitment to the ultimate goals of high achievement for all students. To that end, this book provides an outstanding over-view of the key issues in inclusive assessment for *all* students, regardless of issues of dis-ability or language and culture. For example, Chapters 3 and 4, on the use of accommoda-tions, provide a layperson's interpretation of much of the current research in the context of policy imperatives, but they assume the policymaker or practitioner has basic skills that allow meaningful application—the materials are in no way "dumbed down"! Given that the book provides powerful and varied resources to consult for more information, there is an opportunity to build an understanding that may not currently be in place. It may be that a study group approach to really mining the resources, which builds a common understand-ing among practitioners and key stakeholders, would be a powerful way to create local capacity to do this well. The book provides a unique "one-stop shop" for including students with disabilities and English language learners (ELLs), as well as students with disabilities who are *also* ELLs, in large-scale assessments. This is a great opportunity for a local study group to compare and contrast how varying student needs guide accommodations choices.

The nuances of accommodations issues are challenging, whether for scaffolding instruc-tion or for assessing learning for purposes of a standards-based reform accountability. The issues require a deep understanding of the content to be taught and assessed—something not all special education-trained teachers have. It is absolutely essential that any application of the approaches suggested here be done in a collaborative team context, including per-sonnel knowledgeable in content and in general classroom curriculum and instruction and those with expertise in how learners with unique needs can be instructed in the same chal-lenging content as all other enrolled grade peers. The case studies that serve as examples throughout the book are very helpful, but no single story can give you legs under your learn-ing. Carrying forward the study group idea, it will be important to add your own case studies and collaborate on applying what you learn here to real cases. A local, real-life example is one of the most powerful learning tools you can find, especially with a cross-disciplinary study group team contributing to the solutions.

The information on alternate assessments in this book is less a "how to" and more a discussion of the complexities of building such alternatives for the purpose of system accountability, generally a state responsibility. This accurately reflects the infancy of a most promising and interesting field. A study group needs to grapple with how to teach the challenging content to *all* students, including those with the most significant cognitive disabilities or others who cannot show what they know on a traditional pencil-and-paper test. To that end, an additional website that provides easily accessible white papers, research, and instructional examples is provided by the National Alternate Assessment Center: *naacpartners. org/products.aspx*.

Ultimately these two assessment professionals come full circle. The discussion in Chapters 6–8 about instruction and curriculum is the point of all this assessment talk: testing in the context of standards-based reform is always about improving instruction and access to the challenging general curriculum. Any study group has to start there and carefully consider outdated beliefs and attitudes about what students with disabilities and ELLs *should* be taught and to what level they *should* learn. The authors conclude with a powerful statement of equity and opportunity. It may be that, in the end, not all students will master the full range of knowledge and skills for their grade level. The issue is that we will not know how many or which ones can unless and until we teach (and assess) them all! That, in a nutshell, is what testing for system accountability in standards-based reform, and this wonderful book, are all about.

RACHEL F. QUENEMOEN, MS
Senior Research Fellow
National Center on Educational Outcomes
University of Minnesota

Preface

Over the past 20 years, the standards-based accountability movement has resulted in an increase in the number of assessments administered by states and school districts, with higher stakes attached to test performance for students and educators. Associated with the increased quantity, complexity, and stakes of large-scale assessments is the expectation that these assessments will yield useful information for *all* students, including students with disabilities and English language learners. As a result, educators must prepare students with diverse educational needs to participate successfully in large-scale assessment and accountability programs.

To prepare educators to meet these demands, No Child Left Behind (NCLB) mandated professional preparation and inservice training focused on inclusive instructional and assessment practices. Specifically, NCLB requires state and school districts to provide professional development that focuses on scientifically based instruction for children with special needs and the use of assessment data to inform classroom practice (Title IX, Section 9101[34]). This requirement for assessment-focused professional development reflects national trends toward improving teachers' assessment literacy via state licensure requirements (Stiggins, 1999) and professional standards of practice (Wise, 1996).

Unfortunately, research conducted at the National Center for Research on Evaluation, Standards, and Student Testing suggests that the inability to critically examine and meaningfully apply assessment data is pandemic at all levels of the educational system—from the statehouse to the schoolhouse (Baker, Bewley, Herman, Lee, & Mitchell, 2001; Baker & Linn, 2002). In addition, research by Koretz (1997) indicates that the inclusion of students with diverse needs in state assessments is often plagued by unusual variability in accommodations and assessment practices. In some cases, this variation may reflect a lack of reliable research evidence and professional standards to guide practices, but it also appears that many schools currently lack the capacity to effectively and systematically include students with diverse needs in standards-based accountability (Koretz & Barton, 2003).

To facilitate instructional change and educational improvement, assessments need to be not only valid measures of academic performance but also meaningful and manageable tools for test users (e.g., teachers, administrators, and parents). For this to happen, educators need to develop *assessment literacy*. As defined by Fullan (2003), *assessment literacy* includes (1) the capacity and ability to gather meaningful data regarding student performance; (2) skills to critically analyze and interpret assessment data; (3) the ability to use assessment data to create plans for instructional improvement; and (4) confidence in interpreting, discussing, and (when necessary) debating assessment strategies and the resulting data with the public and policymakers.

This book provides guidance and materials for promoting the inclusion of students with diverse needs in large-scale assessment programs, with a focus on improving access to instruction within the general curriculum for all students. In order for large-scale assessment and accountability programs to lead to enhanced learning for all students, it is important for educators to (1) understand the rationale for developing inclusive accountability systems; (2) hold high expectations for the success of all students; (3) know related federal requirements for students to attain high standards through performance as a part of large-scale assessment programs; (4) recognize the challenges associated with effectively including diverse students in large-scale assessment programs; (5) be familiar with a variety of assessment options for diverse students (i.e., with accommodations and/or through an alternate assessment); (6) effectively distinguish between target and access skills that are relevant to current large-scale testing programs; (7) use an informed framework for making decisions about how to include students with diverse needs; (8) learn how to evaluate whether students have access to instruction in target skills; and (9) design classroom assessment and instruction to be accessible to students with the widest variety of needs, taking into consideration principles of universal design for instruction and assessment. This book is intended to support the development of knowledge and skill in each of these areas among educators and school support personnel.

With this aim in mind, we include a discussion of the rationale and legal basis for inclusive accountability, step-by-step instructions for making participation and accommodation decisions, and user-friendly forms and examples to guide teams through an informed decision-making process. It is important to note that federal and state legislation, as well as state and district accountability practices, are being revised constantly. As a result, some of the legal information we provide may be out of date even by the time our first readers purchase the book. We have done our best to provide guidelines for decision making that are universal; however, it is important to be aware of changes in law that are continually being made over time.

Chapter 1 provides readers with brief historical background of the standards-based reform movement in the United States as well as information on recent legislation (i.e., NCLB and the Individuals with Disabilities Education Improvement Act [IDEA]) and how it relates to diverse groups of students, including students with disabilities and English language learners. The focus of this chapter is on assisting readers in understanding the rationale for developing inclusive large-scale assessment and accountability systems and the importance of making appropriate decisions.

Chapter 2 provides a framework for making decisions about how diverse students participate in large-scale assessment programs. It includes two case studies about students with very different needs and how the team used the described decision-making process to make appropriate participation decisions. The chapter provides an overview of various methods for participation, which are then discussed in more depth in Chapters 3–5.

Chapters 3 and 4 provide detailed information on various accommodations that might be used to facilitate optimal participation among students with disabilities (Chapter 3) and English language learners (Chapter 4) and guidelines for making appropriate decisions to ensure that students receive accommodations that facilitate appropriate measurement of students' skills and knowledge.

Chapter 5 provides information on various formats for alternate assessment that are commonly used to assess skills and knowledge among students with significant cognitive disabilities. A case-based example of how one student was assessed through alternate assessment is also provided.

Chapter 6 describes methods for ensuring that all students have access to the general curriculum. Specific strategies for promoting access are explained. Chapter 7 expands these ideas by providing information on the concept of universal design and how it can be applied to facilitate better instruction and assessment to promote student learning.

Finally, Chapter 8 provides a concluding discussion of the importance of developing inclusive assessment systems and ensuring access to the general curriculum, connecting these practices to professional standards from a variety of organizations.

ACKNOWLEDGMENTS

We would like to thank Craig Thomas, Kenneth Merrell, Diane Browder, and Rachel Quenemoen for their assistance in completing this book.

SARA E. BOLT
ANDREW T. ROACH

Contents

List of Figures, Tables, and Appendices

FIGURES

TABLES

APPENDICES

1

No Child Left Behind
and Standards-Based Reform
and Accountability

This chapter begins by locating inclusive standards-based reform and accountability in historical efforts to improve schooling in the United States of America. Characteristics and components of current assessment and accountability programs are identified and defined. The role of inclusive assessment and accountability in two recent federal policies—No Child Left Behind of 2001 (NCLB) and the Individuals with Disabilities Education Improvement Act (IDEA 2004)—also is discussed. Finally, we set the purpose for the rest of this text, contending that information about and understanding of inclusive standards-based accountability can empower educators to improve educational practices and outcomes for the diverse groups of students attending our nation's schools.

SCHOOL REFORM IN THE UNITED STATES: A BRIEF HISTORY

Americans have a long-standing interest in reforming public education. As early as the 19th century, politicians and intellectuals took an interest in public education as a vehicle for social and economic advancement. In the 1830s, Horace Mann spearheaded the creation of the Massachusetts State Board of Education, subsequently serving as the first Secretary of the Board. As Board Secretary, Mann instituted numerous educational reforms including conducting rigorous evaluations of the condition of the common schools, creating institutes for training teachers, increasing the length of the school year, and lobbying for funding to increase teacher salaries, buy materials, and construct new schools. In addition, Mann pursued the implementation of "moral training" for students, standardization of curricula, and skills-focused classroom instruction (Mondale & Patton, 2002).

By the beginning of the 20th century, the industrial revolution had placed new pressures on a variety of social institutions, including public schools. Rather than the one-room schoolhouses that were common in more agrarian communities, urban schools often had hundreds of students assigned to multiple teachers and classrooms. In response to these social changes, reformers such as Ellwood Cubberley sought to apply new organizational structures to education. Using industrial management theory, Cubberley established an educational administrative system that was led by a professional class of superintendents and principals. This hierarchical model of professionalized school leadership became the standard for educational systems and persists today (Mondale & Patton, 2002).

The Sputnik crisis of the late 1950s initiated multiple waves of school reform efforts that have produced (at best) uneven results. Threatened by the success of the Soviet space program, the federal government invested substantial resources to improve mathematics and science education. Subsequent programs (e.g., Head Start, Upward Bound) included resources for compensatory education to improve academic and vocational outcomes for minority students and students living in poverty.

Over the last half-century, university-based researchers and policymakers have become increasingly adept and prolific at creating model programs for the development of literacy skills, mathematics skills, social behavior, and other valued educational outcomes. Unfortunately, researchers and policymakers' understanding of diffusion, implementation, and institutionalization of school reform programs remains less developed. Reform programs often were universally mandated and initiated (e.g., whole language, "new" math) without the provision of sufficient resources and training to educators. As a result, many reform programs have been less than successful, contributing to decreased confidence in public schools on the part of communities and policymakers and sagging morale among educators.

A Focus on Closing the Gaps

Clearly, one of the long-standing objectives of school reform has been to close the gaps between (1) actual and expected levels of student performance and (2) the performance of the lowest achieving students (or classrooms or schools) and the overall level of achievement for the entire population. A focus on reducing these gaps, according to Fullan (2003), can provide school systems with moral purpose (or what complexity theorists call a "social attractor") that informs and drives reform efforts. This logic has been embraced by supporters of inclusive education and universal design of learning, who have suggested ensuring access and improved outcomes for students with disabilities and English language learners (ELLs) can result in improved services to all students (Capper, Frattura, & Keyes, 2000; O'Brien & O'Brien, 1995; Roach & Frank, 2007).

Designing and implementing school reform to close the gaps, however, necessitates focusing the educational system's attention and limited resources (e.g., instructional time, financial support, or professional development) on students, classrooms, and schools where there is the greatest need (O'Day, 2002). To facilitate these efforts, educators and policymakers need (1) a clear understanding of the desired outcomes for education systems (e.g., improved student achievement) and (2) access to valid and reliable measures of educational progress and the ability to use these measures to inform and guide their efforts to achieve these outcomes.

The importance of gap-closing reform efforts is illustrated in the results of a recent study of student performance in 32 countries (Organization for Economic Cooperation and Development, 2000). Those countries with the largest gaps in students' achievement demonstrated equally troubling outcomes in a number of other areas (e.g., indices of mental and physical health, competence and coping skills, and workers' skill level and employability). As this study's results suggest, reducing gaps in educational performance might play an important role in promoting social and economic development at the community, state, and national level (Roach & Frank, 2007).

UNDERSTANDING AND IMPLEMENTING STANDARDS-BASED REFORM AND ACCOUNTABILITY

As currently designed and implemented, standards-based assessment and accountability systems (e.g., NCLB) are based on a theory of action that posits increased data about student achievement coupled with incentives for increased performance (and corresponding punishments for lack of improvement) will motivate educators and produce improved student outcomes (Baker & Linn, 2002). Some education researchers have labeled this the "new accountability" and have outlined the following additional components of these systems: (1) the use of student achievement data as an indicator of system and educator functioning; (2) public reporting of student performance data; and (3) utilization of the school as the unit of analysis for reform efforts (Elmore, Abelman, & Fuhrman, 1996; O'Day, 2002; Roach & Frank, 2007).

Some education leaders, however, have suggested that the "new accountability" may be overly simplistic in its understanding of educational reform (Elmore, 2003; Fullan, 2003; O'Day, 2002). One area of difficulty is the validity and utility of the results from educational assessments used in accountability systems. Serious reservations have been raised about using the results of large-scale assessments for (1) monitoring student, classroom, school, and system performance and (2) guiding decision making about curriculum and instruction. For example, one possible negative consequence standards-based reform and accountability is the narrowing of the enacted curriculum and de-emphasis of many important educational experiences (e.g., music, art, athletics, and community services) (Baker & Linn, 2002). Unfortunately, relatively little research is available to demonstrate the instructional utility and effects of large-scale assessment systems. Within the context of high-stakes accountability, policymakers need to identify ways to introduce more meaningful reporting mechanisms to inform educators' and policymakers' decision making. In addition, teachers and other educators (e.g., school psychologists, speech therapists) need to identify or develop classroom-based assessments that can provide them and other stakeholders (students, parents, and administrators) with information that can guide reform efforts.

To support instructional decision making, the assessments used in large-scale assessment and accountability systems need to be technically adequate measures of academic performance and meaningful and manageable tools for test users including teachers, administrators, and parents. Fullan (2003) suggests the public's demand for evidence of increased student learning can serve as an important lever for creating educational reform. For this to happen, however, educators need to develop what Fullan (2003) describes as "assessment literacy," which includes:

- The capacity and ability to gather meaningful data regarding student performance
- The skills to critically analyze and interpret assessment data
- The ability to use assessment data to create plans for instructional improvement
- The confidence in interpreting, discussing, and (when necessary) debating assessment data with the public and policymakers.

Unfortunately, according to research by the National Center for Research on Evaluation, Standards, and Student Testing (CRESST), many educators, administrators, and policymakers have difficulty interpreting and meaningfully applying assessment data (Baker & Linn, 2002; Baker, Bewley, Herman, Lee, & Mitchell, 2001; Roach & Frank, 2007).

In addition to understanding assessment, educators, students, families, and community members must perceive proposed reform targets (e.g., improved student achievement) and the measures of progress toward them as attainable and useful. In other words, when designing and implementing inclusive standards-based reform and accountability systems, "clarity must be achieved on the receiving end more than on the delivery end" (Fullan, 1996, p. 420). Spillane's (1999) research on the implementation of standards-based reform in mathematics illustrates this point. Using an interpretive or "sense-making" framework, Spillane described the school contexts and interactions with colleagues that support teachers' understanding of standards-based reform and integration of it into their existing instructional practices. Spillane found that educators' "zones of enactment" are shaped by (1) their skills, values, and knowledge; (2) the social and professional support available to them in implementing reforms; and (c) the material resources (e.g., curriculum guides, assessment instruments, and policy documents) available to explain and support the proposed reforms. Traditionally, preparation for implementing instructional reforms has focused on providing educators with professional development (usually in one-shot workshops) and incentives to implement new programs. However, Spillane's research (Spillane, 1999; Spillane, Reiser, & Reimer, 2002) suggests educators' capacity and commitment to successfully enact inclusive standards-based reform and accountability depends on whether their "zones of enactment":

- are social rather than individualistic.
- provide opportunities for rich deliberations about the substance of reforms and the practicing of the reform elements with other educators and reform experts (e.g., researchers or consultants).
- include material resources or artifacts that can guide their "sensemaking" about the standards and accountability programs.

Although implementation of some instructional programs may require only superficial or mechanical changes in classroom practice, inclusive standards-based reform and accountability ask educators to make deep, sustained changes to their teaching behaviors and to the beliefs and assumptions underlying them. Therefore, careful consideration of the most appropriate professional preparation, inservice training, and instructional support are essential for its success.

DIFFERENT TYPES OF STANDARDS: CONTENT, PERFORMANCE, AND ACHIEVEMENT

Keeping track of the different types of standards can be difficult for educations and other stakeholders who are interested in understanding and implementing standards-based reform. A useful resource is the *Glossary of Assessment Terms and Acronyms* produced by the Council of Chief State School Officers (2003). This document identifies two types of standards—content and performance—and provides the following definitions:

- *Content standards:* Statements of subject-specific knowledge and skills that schools are expected to teach students, indicating what students should know and be able to do.
- *Performance standards:* Indices of qualities that specify how adept or competent a student demonstration must be and that consist of the following four components: (1) levels that provide descriptive labels or narratives for student performance (i.e., advanced, proficient, etc.); (2) descriptions of what students at each level must demonstrate relative to the tasks; (3) examples of student work at each level illustrating the range of performance within each level; and (4) cut scores clearly separating each performance level (Council of Chief State School Officers, 2003, p. 10).

Readers should note that the NCLB substituted the term *achievement standards* for performance standards. Because of this change in terminology, educators may be confronted with documents that use these terms interchangeably. However, the meaning of these terms is relatively straightforward. Essentially, content standards are statements of *what* students should learn, whereas achievement standards describe *how much* or *how well* students should be able to demonstrate their learning.

Glatthorn, Bragaw, Dawkins, and Parker (1998) suggest that the development of content standards was intended to (1) focus on *what students will do* rather than serve as a description of activities or resources to be used; (2) define skills and concepts in specific subject domains, perhaps to the detriment of interdisciplinary thematic instruction; and (3) delineate a K–12 curriculum where common topics and concepts across grade levels help to create a coordinated or "vertically aligned" educational system. According to the U.S. Department of Education's (2003) *Standards and Assessment Non-Regulatory Guidance*, in grades 3–8, content standards for reading, language arts, and mathematics may be developed for a specific grade or for a cluster of grade levels if differing content expectations are provided for each grade in the cluster. For K–12 science and for high school language arts and mathematics, however, "content standards may be grade specific, may cover more than one grade, or may be course specific" (p. 6).

Most states' content standard documents have a three- or four-level hierarchical structure with the most general level being a *content area or subject domain* (e.g., Language Arts, Mathematics). Each content area comprises multiple *content standards* that subsume

Level 1: Content Area/Subject Domain	Language arts
Level 2: Content Strand/Standard	Reading
Level 3: Competency/Goal	Use word recognition skills and strategies to communicate.
Level 4: Objectives/Performance Indicators	A. Student matches letters and sounds. B. Student matches printed words to objects. C. Student reads and recognizes basic sight words.

FIGURE 1.1. Example of the organization of state content standards.

multiple *goals or competencies,* and in turn, each competency can be further defined by specific *objectives or performance indicators.* Figure 1.1 illustrates the relationship among these four levels of content. Unlike the example, some states' standards documents do not include the competency or goal level, resulting in a three-level structure.

To meet the needs of students with significant cognitive disabilities, many states have also created *extended content standards* or *extended curriculum frameworks.* The purpose of these documents is to move "from grade-level expectations to progressively less complex versions of the standard. This continuum of `entry points' provides a range of options at which a student with disabilities can access the content at an appropriately challenging level" (U.S. Department of Education, 2003, p. 68701). Typically, these documents have embraced the same general organization of standards (Level 2) and goals (Level 3), while including alternate objectives or performance indicators (Level 4) that are intended to be more reasonable and accessible for students with significant cognitive disabilities and/or ELLs. Figure 1.2 provides an illustration of the relationship between general and extended content standards and the accompanying assessment instruments meant to measure students' mastery of this content.

States also are required to develop achievement standards for reading/language arts and mathematics for each grade in elementary and middle school and for the grade 10–12 span in high school. The performance descriptors in these achievement standards must be "content specific and competency based . . . [and] apply to all students, unless alternate achievement standards have been developed for students with the most severe cognitive disabilities" (U.S. Department of Education, 2005, p. 8). For example, achievement standards in reading/language arts would include a description of what behaviors and knowledge would be indicative of "proficient" grade-level reading. For students with significant cognitive disabilities, states can develop alternate achievement standards that are expectations for performance that differ in complexity from a grade-level achievement standard. According to U.S. Department of Education Guidelines, academic and alternate achievement standards must include

1. At least three levels (two indicating high achievement and one indicating basic achievement).
2. Descriptors that clearly define the competencies associated with each level.
3. Cut scores that differentiate between the levels (U.S. Department of Education, 2005, p. 9).

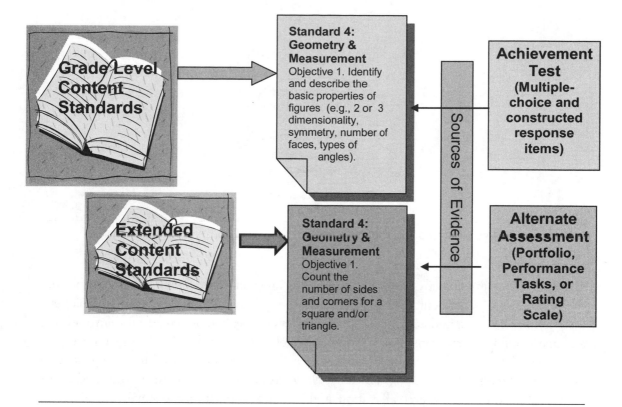

FIGURE 1.2. The relationship between content standards, extended content standards, and assessments. Adapted from Elliott (2006).

Typically, states' achievement standards have been developed by a committee of educators and other stakeholders who have collaborated to develop descriptions of student performance and identify cut scores for students at each achievement level.

Alignment is essential for standards-based reform and accountability. Overload and fragmentation can be major barriers to the implementation of standards-based reform and accountability (Fullan, 1996, 2003). The substance of instructional programs, academic standards, and assessments designed to measure student achievement sometimes contradict each other, which can result in increased stress and pressure for educators and students (Roach, Niebling, & Kurz, 2008). Therefore, pursuing *alignment* of the system's expectations is an important first step to facilitate educational improvement for *all* students (see Figure 1.3). One common definition of *alignment* is the extent "to which expectations and assessments are in agreement and serve in conjunction with one another to guide the system toward students learning what they are expected to know and do" (Webb, 2002, p. 1).

Webb (1997) outlines three approaches to establishing the alignment among curriculum, instruction, and assessment systems: (1) sequential development, (2) expert review, and (3) document analysis. Sequential development involves creation and acceptance of one policy element (e.g., content standards), which subsequently serves as a "blueprint" for the creation of additional policy elements (e.g., instructional materials; assessments). The process of expert review involves the convening of a panel of content experts to review the assessments, content standards, and instruction to determine the extent of their "match" or

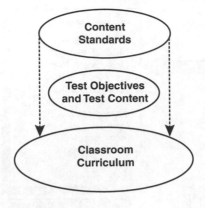

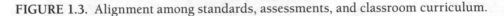

FIGURE 1.3. Alignment among standards, assessments, and classroom curriculum.

alignment. Document analysis involves the coding and analysis of documents that represent the different policy elements. The integration of these three methods allows test developers, instructional leaders, and educational policymakers to create more coherent reform efforts and accountability programs (Roach, Elliott, & Webb, 2005; Webb, 1997). To support standards-based reform and accountability, however, these efforts may need to be expanded to determine the alignment among additional elements and systemic features: pre- and inservice teacher training, resource allocation, and students' opportunity to learn.

NCLB'S INFLUENCE ON STANDARDS-BASED REFORM AND ACCOUNTABILITY

NCLB is a revision and expansion of the Elementary and Secondary Education Act (ESEA). NCLB is the largest federal education funding program in U.S. history and has resulted in a multitude of new requirements, incentives, resources, and challenges for states. With NCLB, the federal government took on a broader and stronger role in education than it did previous versions of ESEA. According the U.S. Department of Education, NCLB is "built on four common-sense pillars: accountability for results, an emphasis on doing what works based on scientific research, expanded parental options, and expanded local control and flexibility" (Essex, 2006, p. 1). This book primarily focuses on assessment and accountability systems, but the other three "pillars" are important influences on inclusive accountability and information relevant to these components also is discussed at various points in this book.

In the arena of state accountability programs, NCLB increased previous assessment requirements and substantially altered the expectations and consequences for student performance. Under previous versions of ESEA, states were required to develop educational standards and to test students in at least one elementary, middle school, and high school grade annually (e.g., grades 4, 8, and 10). In addition, states could determine the assessments, the subject matter assessed, expectations for student and school performance, and what to do about schools not meeting expectations.

NCLB is more expansive, and explicit, in defining assessment and accountability than previous legislation. Among the most important changes are the following:

- States must conduct annual assessments of students' reading/language arts and mathematics performance in grades 3–8, and at least one grade in high school, by the 2005–2006 school year. In addition, an annual science assessment must be implemented in at least one elementary, middle school, and high school grade by the 2007–2008 school year.

- The reading achievement of students who have attended schools in the United States for 3 or more consecutive years must be assessed using tests written and administered in English. In addition, states and schools must conduct annual assessments of the English language proficiency of all limited-English-proficient (LEP) students.

- *Adequate yearly progress* (AYP) is defined as progress toward meeting the goal of 100% of all children in a state achieving "proficiency" on state assessments by the 2013–2014 school year. States are required to set intermediate goals or performance targets for schools that will results in all students achieving proficient performance by 2013–2014. Other indicators (e.g., attendance) may also be used to track schools' progress, but improved student performance (as measured by standards-focused assessments) is considered the most important goal.

- States, school districts, and schools are required to assess, monitor, and meet AYP for identifiable subgroups, including groups defined by race/ethnicity, socioeconomic standing, gender, disability status, and English language proficiency. States, districts, and schools also are required to include at least 95% of the students in each category participate in annual assessments. This disaggregation of performance by subgroups results in a matrix of 37 cells for student performance determinations at each grade level tested. An example of this matrix is provided in Figure 1.4. Failure to meet AYP targets for any of the subgroups (i.e., in any of the cells) can result in a school being identified as "in need of improvement."

- Federal funds can be withheld from states failing to meet progress and inclusion requirements, and states must provide resources and "corrective action" to schools failing to meet AYP for two consecutive years (i.e., identified as "in need of improvement"). Schools identified as needing improvement for more than two consecutive years may be restructured in major ways (e.g., reconstitution as a charter school).

- States must inform families and other stakeholders of every district and school's AYP status, including information on test results, test participation rates, attendance, and graduation rates for the total population at each grade level and various subgroups.

- Parents of children in schools needing improvement must be provided with the opportunity (including free transportation) to transfer to a district school meeting AYP. Districts must also provide supplemental services (e.g., private tutoring) for economically disadvantaged students attending schools identified as "in need of improvement" for more than 1 year.

- Schools in need of improvement must develop plans to improve, and those plans must incorporate instructional strategies from "scientifically based research." These schools also must spend at least 10% of NCLB funds on professional development.

	Reading/Language Arts		Mathematics		
	Participation Rate %	Students Proficient %	Participation Rate %	Students Proficient %	Other Academic Indicator*
All Students					
Economically Disadvantaged					
Racial/Ethnic Group 1					
Racial/Ethnic Group 2					
Racial/Ethnic Group 3					
Racial/Ethnic Group 4					
Racial/Ethnic Group 5					
Students with Disabilities					
ELL Students					

FIGURE 1.4. Example of the 37 student performance determinations. "Other academic indicator" is typically attendance for grades 3–8 and graduate rate at high school. From U.S. Department of Education (2003).

IDEA'S MANDATE FOR INCLUSIVE STANDARDS-BASED REFORM AND ACCOUNTABILITY

IDEA 2004 clearly mandates that students with disabilities should have access to the general education curriculum and academic standards. Specifically, students' individualized education programs (IEPs) must include consideration of how the student will access the general education curriculum (§1414[d]). Moreover, this section of IDEA requires that all students have opportunities and instruction that allow them to make progress toward state and district academic standards.

Although each student with a disability has the legal right to individually referenced curriculum and instruction, outcomes linked to the general education program have become the optimal target. Therefore, educators and families must understand that physical presence in mainstreamed settings does not meet the spirit of IDEA and NCLB. Students with disabilities must be provided with instructional supports and accommodations that promote their progress, no matter how modest, toward the educational expectations of the larger student population (Pugach & Warger, 2001; Roach & Elliott, 2006).

Although standards-based reform and accountability represent a promising strategy to increase access to the general curriculum and academic progress for students with disabilities and ELLs, it is not without challenges or risks. If students with disabilities and ELLs are not provided access adequate opportunities to learn the skills and concepts on standards-focused alternate assessments, their diminished performance may be viewed by some educators as causing schools', districts', and states' inability to reach AYP targets. To address this need, additional information on providing access to the general curriculum is Chapter 6 of this book.

RESPONDING AND COPING WITH STANDARDS-BASED REFORM AND ACCOUNTABILITY: KNOWLEDGE IS POWER!

In a recent analysis of the NCLB, Roach and Frank (2007) applied Ritzer's (2000) McDonaldization thesis to understand the purposes and consequences of standards-based reform and accountability. Ritzer suggested that the majority of modern organizations and systems increasingly are governed by the basic tenets of rationality and scientific management. He identified a familiar modern organization—McDonald's—whose structures and practices illustrate and exemplify rationality and scientific management in action. He then used McDonald's as an exemplar for changes in other modern organizations, including schools. According to Ritzer, McDonaldized systems and routines are characterized by four central features: (1) a pursuit of efficiency; (2) emphasis on calculability or quantification of outcomes; (3) predictability and uniformity of practices; and (4) control through nonhuman technologies (like reporting large-scale assessments).

Roach and Frank's (2007) analysis examined how the central features of McDonaldization are prevalent in current large-scale assessment and accountability systems in education like NCLB. They concluded their critique by applying some of Ritzer's (2000) ideas for coping with and resisting standards-based reform and accountability systems increasing influence on schools and classrooms. Roach and Frank's suggestions include:

1. Educators should attempt to mitigate the worst aspects of NCLB by emphasizing to families and other stakeholders that large-scale assessments are only one index of student and school performance. Moreover, educators should take the lead in identifying and collecting more appropriate and useful data to demonstrate the effectiveness of educational programs.

2. Educators should encourage and support innovative practices and programs in their schools. "One-size-fits-all" programming is unlikely to result in improved performance for all students. Moreover, standardized, "teacher-proof" curricula and instruction runs counter to the individualized modifications and scaffolding that many students need to be successful.

3. Educators must be willing (and encouraged) to "speak truth to power." NCLB and large-scale assessment programs support centralized (i.e., federal) power and decision making. In some cases, this centralization may result in greater equity across states, districts, and schools, but it also limits individual educators' and schools' creativity and responsiveness to local needs.

Like Roach and Frank's suggestions, this book is based on the assumption that "knowledge is power." Educators who work with students with disabilities and ELLs often have been uninformed, or misinformed, about standards-based reform and accountability systems. Because of limited knowledge and resources, educators may experience unintended consequences (e.g., narrowing of curriculum, increased stress) of these reforms, rather than the intended consequences (e.g., improved student performance, clear instructional targets). The remaining chapters of this book are intended to assist educators in facilitating realization of the intended consequences of inclusive standards-based reform and accountability systems by making better, more-informed decisions about how to respond to the demands of these reforms, particularly as they relate to students with diverse needs.

2

Making Participation Decisions for Diverse Students

The federal mandate for *all* students to be included in large-scale assessment and accountability programs is now clear. All students have a right to the intended benefits of improved teaching and learning that are an anticipated outcome of the standards-based reform movement. However, what remains somewhat unclear is how to best include diverse students, given their unique characteristics and the many challenges associated with assessing their skills and knowledge. Deciding how an individual student will participate in large-scale assessment and accountability is extremely important because of how it relates to the instruction later provided to help the student meet proficiency standards as measured by the selected assessment option. This chapter is intended to provide a broad overview of (1) the participation options typically available for students with disabilities and ELLs and (2) a process to guide participation decision making for individual students. More detailed information on the various participation options are included in the chapters that follow.

WHAT DOES FEDERAL LEGISLATION SAY ABOUT OPTIONS FOR PARTICIPATION?

One of the goals of educational accountability is to have accurate information on the academic progress of the entire student population. In order for schools and districts to meet federal requirements for demonstrating AYP, *all* students must participate in the state (or districtwide) assessment program. Although there is some flexibility such that schools and districts can meet federal requirements with a 95% participation rate, it is anticipated that 100% participation will be sought such that the resulting scores will reflect the achievement of the entire student population. Students who are repeatedly absent on testing days and on test make-up days might be part of the remaining untested 5%.

Most students are expected to participate in the general large-scale assessment. However, some students with disabilities and ELLs may not be able to demonstrate their skills and knowledge effectively on the general assessment. In these cases, appropriate accommodations may be provided or the student may participate in an alternate assessment, as determined by the IEP team. Accommodations are changes in how a test is presented, responded to, scheduled, or the setting in which it takes place, such that the change allows for the measurement of the intended skills and knowledge among students with unique needs (Burns, 1998). An alternate assessment involves using a different method or different test to measure students' skills and knowledge (Thompson, Quenemoen, Thurlow, & Ysseldyke, 2001) and is more commonly used to assess students with disabilities than those who are solely ELLs.

Federal legislation allows states to develop three different types of alternate assessments for students with disabilities. These include (1) alternate assessment toward grade-level achievement standards, (2) alternate assessment toward modified standards, and (3) alternate assessment toward alternate achievement standards. Any number of students can participate in these alternate assessment types; however, only a certain percentage of students can be considered "proficient" via certain alternate assessment methods. The proportion of students that can be considered "proficient" according to an alternate assessment toward alternate achievement standards is limited to 1% of all students, and the proportion of students that can be considered "proficient" according to an alternate assessment toward modified achievement standards is limited to 2% of all students. Given these apparent caps on the percent that can be considered proficient, it is anticipated that only the respective proportion of students with disabilities will participate in the alternate assessments toward modified or alternate achievement standards. Table 2.1 presents the associated expectations for how students with disabilities would be expected to participate.

There are also some federal requirements related to participation options for ELL students. For the most part, ELL students are expected to participate in the same assessment program as all other students and have their performance count in determining AYP. However, ELLs can be excluded from participating in the reading/English language arts section of the assessment program during their first year of enrollment in U.S. public schools. ELLs can participate in the English/language arts section of the assessment program in their native language. However, after 3 years of enrollment in U.S. public schools they are expected to participate in this section in English, although exceptions can be made on an individual student basis for an additional 2 years. ELLs are allowed to participate in other

TABLE 2.1. Expected Participation Rates of All Students and Students with Disabilities in the Various Assessment Options

Assessment option	Percent of All Students	Percent of Students with Disabilities
Regular assessment		
Regular assessment with accommodations	97	~63
Alternate assessment toward grade-level achievement standards		
Alternate assessment toward modified standards	2	~18
Alternate assessment toward alternate achievement standards	1	~9

sections of the testing program (e.g., math, science) in their native language as long as it is deemed appropriate. Furthermore, the performance of ELLs who exit out of receiving services for Limited English Proficiency (LEP) can be counted as part of the disaggregated group of LEP students for up to 2 years after they finish receiving services. In addition to participating in testing that is used to determine adequate yearly progress, ELLs must also take an English language proficiency test on an annual basis.

VARIATION ACROSS THE 50 STATES

The requirements listed above play out in different ways across different states. In order to know what the related rules and participation options are in your state, search your state education agency's website or contact someone at the state education agency directly. Some states only have one or two types of alternate assessments (Thompson, Johnstone, Thurlow, & Altman, 2005). Furthermore, the accommodations that are allowed for different groups of students tend to vary considerably across states. In some states (e.g., Oregon), accommodations are available to all students who are considered to need them as opposed to just students with disabilities and ELLs. Your state may have particular guidelines that will help you determine how a particular student should participate in the assessment program used for accountability purposes. The following guidelines can be considered best practice that may or may not already be outlined in information provided to IEP teams in your state.

MAKING PARTICIPATION DECISIONS ON AN INDIVIDUAL BASIS

For students with disabilities, federal law requires that the IEP team determines how individual students will participate. It is important for teams to consider the student's individual needs in making these decisions (Fuchs, Fuchs, & Capizzi, 2005). For ELLs, there is no requirement related to who makes the decision, unless the ELL is also a student with a disability, in which case the IEP team determines how the ELL will participate. However, it is advised that decisions for all ELLs are made according to a similar process, given that each ELL may have very different characteristics and testing needs. In making decisions, teams should follow federal and state requirements and guidelines; however, the ultimate decision is delegated to a team of individuals that know the student well. Clear decision-making procedures and documentation are important to ensure that the assessment program works well for students with diverse needs (Thompson, Thurlow, Quenemoen, Esler, & Whetstone, 2001; Ysseldyke, Thurlow, McGrew, & Shriner, 1994).

IEP teams who make participation and accommodation decisions typically consist of general and special educators, family members, other educational specialists, and the student (Fuchs et al., 2005). Each of these people brings very valuable contributions to the decision-making process, and it is important that each team member's suggestions and concerns be taken into consideration when making a participation decision. Family members and students bring information about their expectations for what the student should ultimately learn in school, which can influence the standards to which the team determines the student should work, and therefore how the student is assessed. Whenever possible, the student should also provide information about what changes are helpful to him or her when being tested. When students are included in the decision-making process, they may be much more likely to follow through with the team's recommendations. General education teachers can bring to the team knowledge about the grade-level content standards, which represent what students are to be taught and what is to be assessed. Special educators can bring to the team knowledge of methods for making instruction and testing more accessible to students with unique needs, as well as information about methods for alternate assessment. Other specialists, such as school psychologists, social workers, and speech–language pathologists might bring to the team other information on the unique characteristics of the student or knowledge of assessment methods and purposes that may be helpful in making participation decisions.

Although there is not a legally mandated group of individuals responsible for making decisions about how individual ELLs without disabilities will participate in assessment systems, it would be beneficial to consult a variety of individuals in making participating decisions for each ELL. Family members and the student may have different expectations for the student to learn English compared to that of the school. Furthermore, ELLs who have been attending U.S. public schools for similar amounts of time may have different levels of English proficiency and therefore may need different accommodations. It is important to note that there are also many students who are ELLs and students with disabilities. The IEP teams for these students must be sure to take into consideration the given IEP/LEP student's language needs and the unique characteristics of his or her disability when making participation decisions.

It is important to recognize that participation decisions should be tailored to particular content areas (Thurlow, Elliott, & Ysseldyke, 2003). Some students with disabilities may be working toward different standards in different content areas. Different accommodations may be more or less appropriate for them in specific content areas. Furthermore, students can participate in an assessment program in different ways for different content areas. For example, a student might participate in the alternate assessment for English/language arts but take the regular test with accommodations for math. A different level of English proficiency may be needed for ELLs to be successful in different content areas, and so it may be necessary to have them participate in different ways on different content area tests, as well.

Below we provide a set of steps to guide participation decision making. Figure 2.1 provides an illustration of these steps.

Step 1: Ensure That All Decision Makers Understand the Purpose of the Accountability Assessment

In order to make appropriate participation decisions, all those involved in decision making should clearly understand the purpose of participation in the statewide assessment. An understanding of the assessment's purpose is important to developing an understanding of the need for full participation (Almond, Quenemoen, Olsen, & Thurlow, 2000). It should be clearly communicated to all participants that the assessment results are (1) intended to

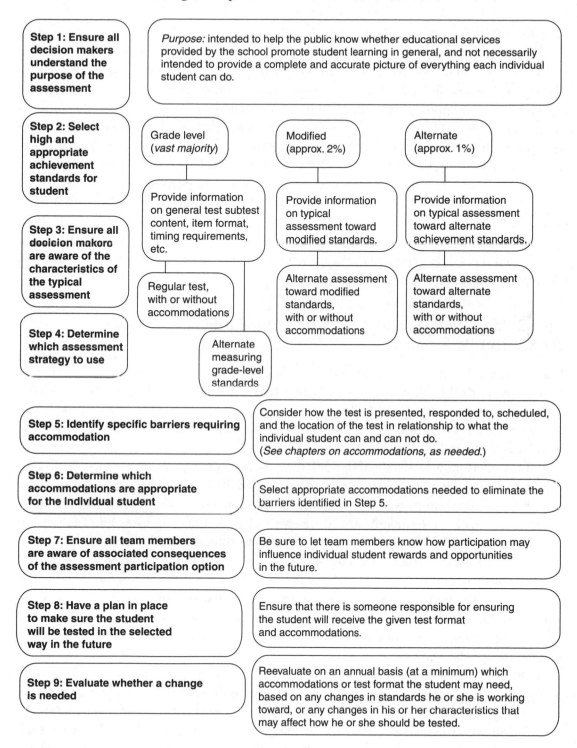

Step 1: Ensure all decision makers understand the purpose of the assessment

Purpose: intended to help the public know whether educational services provided by the school promote student learning in general, and not necessarily intended to provide a complete and accurate picture of everything each individual student can do.

Step 2: Select high and appropriate achievement standards for student

Grade level (*vast majority*)

Modified (approx. 2%)

Alternate (approx. 1%)

Provide information on general test subtest content, item format, timing requirements, etc.

Provide information on typical assessment toward modified standards.

Provide information on typical assessment toward alternate achievement standards.

Step 3: Ensure all decision makers are aware of the characteristics of the typical assessment

Regular test, with or without accommodations

Alternate assessment toward modified standards, with or without accommodations

Alternate assessment toward alternate standards, with or without accommodations

Step 4: Determine which assessment strategy to use

Alternate measuring grade-level standards

Step 5: Identify specific barriers requiring accommodation

Consider how the test is presented, responded to, scheduled, and the location of the test in relationship to what the individual student can and can not do. (*See chapters on accommodations, as needed.*)

Step 6: Determine which accommodations are appropriate for the individual student

Select appropriate accommodations needed to eliminate the barriers identified in Step 5.

Step 7: Ensure all team members are aware of associated consequences of the assessment participation option

Be sure to let team members know how participation may influence individual student rewards and opportunities in the future.

Step 8: Have a plan in place to make sure the student will be tested in the selected way in the future

Ensure that there is someone responsible for ensuring the student will receive the given test format and accommodations.

Step 9: Evaluate whether a change is needed

Reevaluate on an annual basis (at a minimum) which accommodations or test format the student may need, based on any changes in standards he or she is working toward, or any changes in his or her characteristics that may affect how he or she should be tested.

FIGURE 2.1. Steps to guide participation decision making.

help the public know whether educational services provided by the school promote student learning in general and (2) not necessarily intended to provide a complete and accurate picture of all each individual student can do. The purpose of the test is, however, to identify the extent to which individual students are meeting specific academic standards, such that resources can be appropriately allocated to ensure that all students meet the standards in the future. It should be clear to all members of the team that poor performance of the student on the test may actually result in more attention and resources being provided to the student in the future rather than less. Often, we have seen teams make poor participation decisions because members do not understand this ultimate purpose of the test and have instead made decisions based on the assessment option for which they believe the student could achieve the highest score. This is *not* the correct way to determine participation, and actually may *harm* rather than benefit the student in the future. With an appropriate understanding of the purpose of the assessment, team members will be ready to make more appropriate participation decisions.

Step 2: Identify High and Appropriate Standards for Student Performance

One of the most important aspects of the standards-based reform movement is the articulation of standards that all students are anticipated to meet. All students, even those with the most significant and severe disabilities, are expected to have access to instruction and learning according to challenging standards, and to have their progress toward learning those standards measured on a regular basis.

It is important to understand the difference between two primary dimensions of standards, namely content and achievement standards (additional information on the different types of standards was provided in Chapter 1). State content standards represent the broad standards in which *all* students are to receive instruction and be assessed. The general curriculum includes a sequence intended to promote student learning toward the content standards. All students, including those with the most significant disabilities are to be given access to instruction in the content standards for their grade level. For a long time, many students with disabilities were not provided access to instruction in the grade-level content standards; the standards-based reform movement and associated legislation have provided greater opportunities for students with disabilities to receive instruction that address these content standards.

The increased emphasis on providing instruction to all students in the same content standards is creating opportunities for teachers to adapt instruction to include a variety of students in learning the same concepts. In the past, students with very significant disabilities may have only been exposed to instruction associated with grade-levels far below their current grade. Having limited decoding and reading comprehension skills, these students might never have been exposed to the concepts covered in a 10th-grade U.S. history class. Now, general and special education teachers are expected to work together to provide such students access to this high-level content. In many cases, access to the content standards can be provided while a student is working toward developing other skills that are considered more functional than academic in nature (Spooner & Browder, 2006). For instance, it may be the case that a student with very substantial education needs is learning how to use a switch to communicate. Instead of simply using a switch to communicate a desire for a certain type of food, the student might learn to use the switch to communicate which U.S. president he or she would like to have more information about. Some additional examples of how content standards that are used to guide instruction for all students might be incorporated into the instructional activities for students with very significant disabilities are presented in Table 2.2. This topic will also be more fully discussed in Chapter 6.

Although all students are expected to have access to instruction and assessment in the *content* standards, not all students are expected to attain the same standards of *achievement*. Achievement standards represent a particular predetermined level of performance associated with the content standards. For example, if a content standard "will be familiar with the general era in which each U.S. president served," an associated achievement standard might be "identifies the decade in which given U.S. presidents served with 80% accuracy." Although the majority of students with disabilities are anticipated to be instructed toward proficiency in grade-level achievement standards, some may be instructed and learn toward modified or alternate achievement standards, either in some or all academic areas. A decision about whether a student should work toward modified or alternate achievement standards needs to be made very carefully and with due consideration of the associated consequences. In some places, graduation or diplomas may only be awarded to those students who work toward and achieve grade-level achievement standards.

TABLE 2.2. Content-Standard Access Examples for Students with Significant Cognitive Disabilities

Content standard	Activity to address content standard
Describe how people plan for, and respond to, natural disasters	The student is taught to pair given pictures of a fire, tornado, and blizzard with a picture of him or her responding appropriately (i.e., leaving the building in case of fire, sitting in the basement for a tornado, staying inside next to a fire for a blizzard).
Describe and locate the major natural and human features that define places and regions in the United States	The student is taught to pair verbally communicated regions of the United States (e.g., Midwest, New England, Southwest) to locations on a map.
Interpret the relationship between data suggested by tables/ matrices, equations, or graphs	When presented a graph, the student is taught to point to more and less as it is represented in various ways on the graph.
Sing/play major and minor scales	The student is taught to respond in a certain way to a major or minor scale (e.g., with a smile for a major scale or a frown for a minor scale).

How can educators determine which achievement standards should be the focus of a student's classwork and instructional experiences? First, it is very important to be sure that the student does have access to instruction and learning in the grade-level content standards, no matter what his or her level of performance is. Also, for nearly all students, it is anticipated that they will work toward grade-level achievement standards. Only those with very significant cognitive disabilities are considered to be in need of alternate achievement standards set based on what a team determines are appropriate high expectations for them (< 1% of the entire student population). Next, for some students, teams might determine that their rates of learning are such that the number of grade-level achievement standards and objectives should be reduced in order to effectively promote teaching and learning for the student. However, only if the state has specific instruction toward modified standards as an option would it be possible to designate the student to receive instruction focused only on such modified standards. Less than 2% of the entire student population is anticipated to require instruction toward modified achievement standards.

In making participation decisions, it is important to place the focus on maintaining high expectations, regardless of the student's current performance level. A substantial foundation of empirical support exists that examines the influence of teacher's expectations on student achievement; in several cases, low expectations have been shown to lead to limited achievement (Brophy, 1983). It can unfortunately be easy to fall into the practice of making decisions about participation based on the type of assessment on which it is anticipated the student currently would perform well. Although everyone wants to see students perform well, it is important that this desire does not serve as a barrier to students accessing instruction that will challenge them to attain high standards. It is important to recognize that assessment participation decisions are intended to guide future instructional practice. When it is determined that assessment toward modified or alternate achievement standards is necessary, this will put the student on a somewhat different "track" for learning and instruction such that he or she may never attain grade-level achievement standards. This is why federal requirements limit the proportion of students that can be considered proficient according to modified and alternate achievement standards.

Step 3: Ensure That All Decision Makers Are Familiar with Characteristics of the General Assessment

Prior to making decisions about how a student will participate, it is important that all team members are familiar with characteristics of the general large-scale assessment. Without this information, team members may not be able to evaluate whether the test is appropriate for measuring the given student's skills, and whether standard administration of the test might pose any barriers for the student in demonstrating knowledge and skill. Some state education agencies post example test items on their websites, or allow individuals to examine previous versions of the tests used for accountability purposes. By examining sample tests, all team members can get a better idea of what skills and behaviors are required for the student to demonstrate his or her knowledge in the given format. Sometimes, team members have very limited understanding of what the test is actually like and may have developed notions about what it is like based on what they hear in the media or from other individuals. It is important that educators, family members, students, and other team members have correct information about the test.

At this stage, it is important that team members do not consider the *level of perceived difficulty* when examining the test. Instead, they should focus attention on test characteristics associated with the skills needed for the student to effectively demonstrate his or her knowledge on the test. The team should be thinking about characteristics of how student progress toward standards is measured through regular assessment and whether that measurement approach is appropriate for the student, or whether alternative methods are necessary for the student to show knowledge and skill. At this step, the team has already decided which standards are appropriate, and so level of difficulty should not be a factor. Characteristics of the test are being analyzed simply to determine whether it is possible for the student to demonstrate knowledge and skill according to the given assessment format.

Step 4: Determine Which Measurement Strategy to Use

After the team has determined the most appropriate achievement standards for the student to work toward and consequently to be instructed in, and have a good understanding of how the general large-scale assessment is used to measure achievement toward those standards, it is possible to move forward to determine exactly how achievement toward those standards can best be assessed. Assessment programs are designed at the state and district level, and so it is important to become familiar with the policies and practices that are current in your state. Links to many related state assessment program policies can be found through the website for the National Center on Educational Outcomes (*education.umn.edu/nceo/StatePolicies.html*).

It is anticipated that the vast majority of students with disabilities and ELLs will be included in the regular assessment with or without accommodations, and that very few will need to participate in an alternate assessment. For students who are anticipated to work toward the full set of grade-level achievement standards, it is usually determined that they will participate in the regular assessment with or without accommodations. This assessment usually involves administration of a standardized test to determine the extent to which students are meeting grade-level achievement standards. Some states have developed tests based on items from existing published tests that are selected to be appropriate in measuring their given achievement standards. Others have contracted with test publishers to develop their own tests. Still others have involved educators in the actual development of new items and tests. Tests that are used for the regular assessment programs often include a variety of different item types. They may include multiple choice items, constructed response items, and essay items. The way that the tests are designed may make it difficult for some students to demonstrate their achievement of the standards. For instance, multiple choice items may require the student to be able to read lengthy item stems and responses that are presented in English. Essay items may require that students can write legibly and in a relatively brief amount of time. For students with reading disabilities, ELLs, and students with fine motor difficulties, these item characteristics may prevent them from being able to demonstrate their knowledge and skill with respect to what is intended to be measured. In such cases, accommodation(s) may be needed for students to be able to appropriately demonstrate their knowledge and skill toward grade-level achievement standards.

If a student is not able to demonstrate knowledge and skill using the regular assessment even with accommodations, an alternate assessment may be used to assess their knowledge and skill toward grade-level achievement standards (see Chapter 5 for more information). Depending on the type of assessment tactics used, students who participate in alternate assessments might also receive accommodations on the alternate assessment, if it is determined that the accommodations are important for the student to be able to show his or her achievement on the given alternate assessment.

Although states are expected to develop alternate assessments for those who cannot participate in the regular assessment with or without accommodations, they do not necessarily need to develop alternate assessments toward modified or alternate achievement standards, and so it is important to know the alternate assessment options available within your state. Within states that decide to develop alternate assessments toward modified and/ or alternate achievement standards, there is typically reduced depth and/or breadth in the achievement standards measured through the assessment. Consequently, there is substantial variability in how achievement toward these standards is assessed.

Step 5: Consider Potential Barriers to Appropriate Measurement of Target Skills

Once a team has decided which type of assessment is most appropriate for the student to demonstrate his or her skills and knowledge, it is important to consider whether there are any characteristics of the test administration process that may make it particularly difficult for the student to demonstrate his or her knowledge according to the target content and achievement standards. Tests are typically designed such that the majority of students can effectively demonstrate their knowledge and skill with respect to what is intended to be measured. However, students with certain characteristics may have particular difficulties showing what they know and can do on a given test. Just as certain door handles make it difficult for individuals who do not have the ability to twist their hands to open a door to enter a room, so it is often the case that the way that a test is designed fails to allow some students the opportunity to demonstrate their knowledge and skill with respect to what is intended to be measured.

For example, many statewide tests are currently presented in printed format, regardless of whether they are intended to measure students' reading decoding skills. A certain level of reading skill may be needed for students to be able to demonstrate their math, social studies, and science skills on the associated tests. Without the needed reading skills, student performance will likely be much lower than what it could be if the test was offered in a different way. Furthermore, most tests are only available in English or in a few other languages. Students who don't speak English or one of these other languages may not be able to show what they truly know and can do with respect to what is intended to be measured.

However, unlike the clear distinctions between the abilities to twist a door knob and enter a room, it can often be difficult to distinguish between abilities needed to access the test, and abilities actually associated with the skills and knowledge intended to be tested. Sometimes the way that the items are presented is very purposeful, and related to the skills and knowledge that the items are intended to measure. For example, an English/language arts test might require that items be presented in a printed form in order to measure actual student reading comprehension as opposed to listening comprehension. However, if the test is intended to also measure other skills and knowledge related to English/language arts, such as ability to critique an author's perspective, or ability to distinguish between different genres of literature, then it could be argued reading decoding should be considered a separate skill that is needed simply to access the skills and knowledge truly intended to be measured.

To identify whether a given characteristic of a test is a barrier to appropriate testing or whether it represents part of what the test is intended to measure, it can be helpful to refer to the specific content and achievement standards that the test has been developed to assess. Ideally, these should be very well articulated so that there is limited ambiguity about what is intended to be measured. Test users and developers can thereby create a list of aspects related to how the test is constructed and presented that may prohibit the student from demonstrating his or her knowledge. This can then be used to guide the selection of possible accommodations for the student, which is described in the following step.

Step 6: Determine Which Accommodations Are Appropriate

Based on the challenges identified within Step 5, the team can then go on to decide how the challenges might be reduced if certain changes are made in how the test is administered. Such changes are often called "accommodations." Some examples include providing extended time on tests not intended to measure speed with which students can complete the various items, having a test proctor read aloud test items, providing an interpreter for the test, or allowing students to type their answers on a word processor rather than handwrite responses to essay items.

There can be much debate about whether accommodations are appropriate, given that there is often a desire to maintain consistency in how the test is administered to ensure that no student has a special advantage. However, it is important to recognize that as long as the purpose of the test is simply to measure achievement relative to a particular academic standard, and not necessarily to compare scores among students, the need to maintain consistency in how the test is administered may not be so important. What is most important is that in whatever way the test is administered, measurement of the extent to which the student has met the given content and achievement standards is facilitated. Given that different students have different characteristics that may, depending on how the test is typically administered, hinder their demonstration of knowledge and skill, it seems appropriate to change the test administration procedures to meet the needs of students rather than prohibit their access to demonstrating what they know and can do with respect to what is being measured.

There may be a variety of ways that a test can be accommodated to reduce a student-specific challenge identified in Step 4. For instance, a student who is a very slow reader may benefit from extended time, or from having the test read aloud by an assistant, or by having the opportunity to listen to a recorded version of a test. In order to make an appropriate decision about which accommodation to use, it is important to take into consideration the method with which the student is most comfortable and perhaps whether the student frequently uses the given accommodation during instruction (Elliott, Braden, & White, 2001). It also might be important to think about the circumstances under which the student can best demonstrate knowledge. For example, if a student is an extremely slow reader, the student's rate of reading may interfere with his or her comprehension. In such a circumstance, providing a reader or tape recording of the test might be more effective. However, if the student is not used to such accommodations, and can comprehend what he or she reads even when reading at a slow rate, a reader may actually confuse or make it more difficult for the student to show what he or she knows and can do.

In a similar fashion, there may be multiple accommodations possible for ELLs. They might be provided a face-to-face interpreter, a translation, extended time, a dictionary, or a videotaped interpretation of the test. As with the previous example, it is important to consider what the student is used to within his or her instructional programming and which accommodations will make the student feel most comfortable and confident. If the student typically is instructed in English, then it may make sense to simply provide an English version of the test and perhaps slightly more time to process the language, along with a dictionary for any unknown words. If the student is receiving instruction in his or her native language, then an interpreter or a translation might be more appropriate. However, it is important to recognize that translated tests can often differ in difficulty levels; it also can be difficult to ensure that translated tests measure the same construct as the original test (Kopriva, 2000; Salvia, Ysseldyke, & Bolt, 2007).

When possible, it can be very useful to test whether a particular accommodation is truly helpful to the student. Although only a few studies have examined the accuracy with which teachers identify which accommodations are helpful for particular students, available research suggests that teachers are not very accurate in making these predictions (Fuchs, Fuchs, Eaton, Hamlett, & Karns, 2000; Weston, 1999). Hollenbeck (2002) suggested testing whether certain assessment conditions allow for better measurement on an individual student basis. Furthermore, a tool has been developed to more readily enable educators to make accommodation decisions that are supported by empirical data on their effectiveness (Fuchs, Fuchs, Eaton, & Hamlett, 2003).

Once the team has decided which accommodations would best allow the student to demonstrate knowledge and skill, it may be helpful to consult the state policy to determine whether the given accommodations are considered "standard" or "okay." If the given accommodations are not part of the list of accommodations that are considered appropriate according to state policy, the team may need to discuss whether other accommodations that the state policy allows could meet the student's needs in a similar way. If the needs of the student are in conflict with the state accommodation policy, it may be necessary to advocate at the state level for the student to be able to receive the accommodations that the team decided were necessary and appropriate. However, in making a final decision about whether to provide an accommodation, it is important for the team to also take into consideration any associated consequences, which are described in Step 7. More information on accommodations and making decisions about whether to provide accommodations is provided in Chapters 3 and 4.

Step 7: Ensure That All Team Members Are Aware of Associated Consequences of the Assessment Participation Option

In addition to avoiding any negative unintended consequences associated with selecting lower standards than the student may be able to achieve, it is important to ensure that all team members are aware of other consequences associated with different assessment options prior to making a final decision about how the student will participate. In several states, the awarding of regular diplomas is contingent upon scoring at a particular level on the general statewide assessment. If a team decides to have a particular student assessed using the alternate assessment, all team members—including the parents and student—need to be made aware that the decision may prohibit the student from receiving a regular diploma. In some states, certain merit awards may only be available to students who participate in testing in a particular way; parents and students need to be made aware of these conditions when making decisions about test participation. If an accommodation is not considered a "standard" or "okay" accommodation according to the state policy, the student who takes the test with the given accommodation also may not have access to certain merit awards or may not have his or her score count in the same way that it counts for other students.

Step 8: Ensure That There Is a Plan to Follow Through on Testing Day (or during Other Times That Assessment Data Are Collected)

When accommodations are made on an individual basis, it can be very challenging to keep track of the various accommodation packages that students need and to make sure that everything occurs as planned on testing days! (Shriner & DeStefano, 2003). We suggest designating one person within a school as an accommodation coordinator. This person would ensure that the appropriate resources, such as dictionaries, large-print testing booklets, reading assistants, and so forth, are available on testing day to provide accommodations and alternate assessments as listed in each student's plan.

Before testing day, it is important that all individuals who might be assisting with providing accommodations (e.g., those who are reading aloud test items or serving as scribes to write down student responses) are provided appropriate training (Clapper, Morse, Thompson, & Thurlow, 2005). These individuals should have the purpose of the test explained to them and be trained to read items and record student responses exactly as written or spoken. Any elaboration on the part of a reader or scribe may hinder accurate measurement of the student's achievement. Many states have developed training guidelines for these individuals to ensure proper administration of the test. It also is important for reading assistants to know the rules for rereading any items for the student, and to ensure that the items are read at an appropriate pace, given the student's needs.

If alternate assessment involves collection of data across multiple days, it is important to have a clear plan for how and when this data will be collected. It has been recommended that teachers who collect alternate assessment data across multiple days learn to make data collection part of regular instruction. This can assist teachers in making the alternate assessment a more efficient process and allow them to use the data that is collected to potentially inform future instruction as well (Kleinert, Green, Hurte, Clayton, & Oetinger, 2002).

Step 9: Evaluate Whether a Change in Standards and/or Participation Methods Is Needed

In the majority of cases, the most appropriate goal is for students to be able to participate in a regular assessment without needing accommodations and to demonstrate proficiency (or progress toward) grade-level achievement standards. What students currently need generally is not what we want or intend them to need in the future. For example, most students who might receive a read-aloud accommodation due to reading difficulties are also receiving remedial instruction to help them develop better reading skills. Over time, they are expected to acquire the reading skills needed to participate in a statewide assessment without a reader. It is therefore important for the decision-making team to regularly evaluate whether accommodations are still needed. If no longer appropriate or needed, a given accommodation may actually be detrimental to the student's performance on the test. For instance, sometimes a student can more easily reread portions of a test, and wants to easily go back and check his or her own work without the assistance of a reader. The reader may make it difficult for him or her to check over his or her work on a test. It may be important, therefore, to reevaluate accommodation needs as students develop skills. Similarly, as ELLs learn the English language, they may have much less need for tests to be administered in their native language. Given the common difficulties associated with communicating test items in a student's native language, it may be advantageous for a student who is not yet completely proficient in English to be tested in English. It is important that those who know the current functioning of the student help make decisions that will allow for the best measurement strategies possible.

Logistically, it can sometimes be difficult to schedule meetings at a time close to when the statewide assessment is administered. In order to make the most appropriate decisions, it can be valuable to know exactly what skills the student has prior to the time of the test so that appropriate accommodations can be determined. For students who are not receiving special education services, it may be possible to make changes without the need to change legal documents. However, for students who have an IEP, it is important to ensure that what is described on the IEP for statewide testing is what happens on the day of testing.

HOW PARTICIPATION DECISIONS SHOULD *NOT* BE MADE

The above step-by-step process should guide the team toward making an appropriate decision. However, we think that it may be helpful to note here some information that teams may be tempted to use that we consider irrelevant to making appropriate decisions.

Disability Category

There tends to be considerable variation in terms of student characteristics and needs within disability categories, particularly within the 13 federal educational disability categories. Even within more specific categories or diagnoses, such as students with Down syndrome, there are likely some students who can best be tested with the general assessment and some students who can best be tested with an alternate assessment. What is most important to know is the standards to which students are working and how their achievement toward those standards can best be measured.

Restrictiveness of Educational Setting

There also tends to be considerable variation in student characteristics and needs within particular educational placements. Some students who participate in general education classrooms throughout the school day may need an alternate assessment, and some who may be educated in a complete different educational setting may be able to take the regular test without accommodations.

Difficulty Level of the Test

Although it is important for decision makers to review the regular assessment prior to making decisions about how a particular student will participate, it is important that the perceived difficulty level of the test does not become a deciding factor. For there to be accurate information on whether students are meeting the standards selected by the team, it is important that they participate in an associated assessment option.

Fear That the Student Will Not Pass the Test

We have heard of many cases where students have performed better than anticipated on statewide assessment programs. Had it been decided that they should have taken an alternate assessment toward alternate achievement standards, the student may have been a victim of the effects of low expectations. The accountability system is set up to help schools identify where resources may need to be better targeted in order for students to meet standards. If students are systematically excluded because of a concern that they will not pass or demonstrate proficiency, schools will not have the information needed in order to guide decision making about instructional programs and resources.

How the Student Has Participated in the Assessment Program in the Past

As indicated in Step 9 above, students' skills are expected to change, and so their need for various accommodations will change as well. Although probably less common, expectations for students to complete grade-level versus alternate standards may also change over time. It is important to annually evaluate how the student can best participate in the assessment program.

A NOTE ABOUT TEST ANXIETY

Given that tests are being used to make more important decisions about schools and students than ever before, there can be a lot of pressure placed on students to perform well.

Many individuals are concerned that this can result in students feeling very anxious, and some even argue that this potential for heightened anxiety as a result of tests is not worth the data that they may provide. We tend to think that although there are extreme cases in which this may be true, these are very far and few between. For the most part, we believe that tests can provide very important information, and that it is possible to create a school environment in which anxiety associated with testing is minimized. We believe that it is important for school professionals to promote a positive attitude toward testing among their students. Testing is something that will likely continue to be an important part of students' lives as they seek admission to various postsecondary educational settings, and as they are evaluated within work roles in the future. It is important for students to adapt to taking tests in order to be successful throughout their lives.

CASE EXAMPLES

Example 1: Robert

Robert is a third-grade student with severe autism. He has extreme difficulties in completing work independently. He currently receives 1:1 assistance in each of his classes to ensure implementation of a comprehensive behavior management plan and appropriate training in independent functioning. He is very inconsistent in demonstrating knowledge and skill in academic areas. On some class assignments, he scores 100%, and on others, he scores 0%. This is true across content areas, but he does appear to be stronger in mathematics than in English/language arts. He has been observed to read out loud with fluency on occasion. Follow along with Figure 2.2 to see how the team made decisions about how Robert would participate in the statewide assessment program. A blank version of the Participation Decision-Making Form for Students with Disabilities is presented in Appendix 2.1.

Example 2: Julia

Julia is a second-grade student who is an ELL. She has attended Darling Elementary since kindergarten. She is receiving bilingual education (Spanish and English) across her entire school day and has received this type of instruction since she entered kindergarten. Her parents speak only Spanish at home. She can read fluently in Spanish and is just under grade-level benchmarks for reading in English. She typically needs just a little more time to complete classroom assignments and activities in English. She also can become more tired than the typical student when she has to complete activities in English, given the cognitive demands of working in a slightly less familiar language. She is receiving instruction in both languages, and her skills in English are very near grade level. The ultimate goal of her parents and teachers is for her to be able to complete academic activities proficiently in English. They therefore decided to have her participate in the assessment program entirely in English, with extended time and test breaks available to counter her need to have slightly more time for processing the language and accommodate her associated test fatigue. The English as a Second Language (ESL) specialist will be responsible for ensuring that Julia is reminded of and has access to these accommodations on the testing day. The ESL specialist

Participation Decision-Making Form for Students with Disabilities

Is this student also an English language learner (ELL)? <u>No.</u> If yes, complete this form, and then complete the Participation Decision-Making Form for English Language Learners (see Appendix 2.2).

> It may be helpful to attach the following to this form, and provide copies to team members:
> - a copy of the grade-level content, achievement, modified, and alternate achievement standards
> - information on the testing format for the regular assessment and alternate assessment
> - list of accommodations considered standard in your state
> - information on any consequences associated with test participation (e.g., not eligible for merit awards, standard diploma, etc.)
> - an accommodation form to be completed

Student name: <u>Robert Jones</u>　　　Date of birth: <u>October 5, 1999</u>　Grade: <u>3</u>

School: <u>Jefferson Elementary</u>　　　Date form completed: <u>January 9, 2008</u>

Team members participating (their role): <u>Susan and Brian Jones (Robert's parents), Anita Jacobs (Robert's 1:1 assistant), John Smith (general education teacher), Roberta Johnson (special education teacher), Joel Oosterhouse (principal)</u>

Checklist:

X_ All team members have an understanding of the purpose of the accountability assessment

X_ All team members have examined the content standards and grade-level achievement standards

X_ All team members are familiar with the format of the regular assessment

X_ All team members are aware of consequences associated with having the student participate under nonstandard conditions or on an alternate assessment

Brief statement/example of how student is accessing instruction in the content standards: <u>Robert is currently being instructed in the content standards through instruction provided by his general education teacher in the general education classroom for 100% of his school day. He needs regular reminders from his 1:1 assistant to maintain attention to task. Furthermore, he has visual cues that his 1:1 assistant points to on a regular basis to remind him to check over his work. He receives reinforcement every 20 min. that he works independently (with the above-listed accommodations) on written assignments.</u>

High achievement standards selected: *Mark one box for each content area. For any "modified" or "alternate" standards selected, provide brief explanation.*

Content area	Grade level	Modified*	Alternate	Explanation for modified or alternate standards
Math	X			
English/language arts	X			
Social studies	X			
Science	X			

(continued)

FIGURE 2.2. Completed example for Robert of the Participation Decision-Making Form for Students with Disabilities.

*If modified is marked, explain here how standards are being modified: _____

_____

_____

_____

Measurement strategy:

For all content areas above that are marked alternate, plan to administer an alternate assessment toward alternate achievement standards. Examine this alternate assessment format to determine whether accommodations may be needed for the student to access the test. If the student is an English Language Learner (ELL), complete the ELL participation decision-making form (Appendix 2.2). For all students with disabilities, use additional accommodation form to further determine how the student will participate [see Chapter 3].

For all content areas above that are marked modified, plan to administer alternate assessment toward modified standards. Examine the alternate assessment format to determine whether accommodations may be needed for the student to access the test. If the student is an English language learner (ELL), complete the ELL participation decision-making form (Appendix 2.2). For all students with disabilities, use additional accommodation form to further determine how the student will participate [see Chapter 3].

For each content area above that is marked "grade level," plan to administer the regular assessment or an alternate assessment toward grade level standards. Examine the regular format to determine whether accommodations may be needed for the student to access the test. If the student is an English language learner (ELL), complete the ELL participation decision-making form (see Appendix 2.2). For all students with disabilities, use additional accommodation form to further determine how the student will participate [see Chapter 3].

FIGURE 2.2. *(continued)*

will be monitoring Julia's testing session and will ensure that any test breaks that she takes are supervised. The team completed the decision-making form for ELLs as shown in Figure 2.3. A blank version of the form is presented in Appendix 2.2.

THE EVER-EVOLVING NATURE OF STATEWIDE ACCOUNTABILITY SYSTEMS

Statewide assessment programs are quite frequently being revised. In fact, as we wrote this book, many alternate assessment programs were only just being developed. It can often be difficult to be familiar with all of the programs policies that currently apply within your school and district. At the same time, because policies are being shaped in the present, there are many opportunities for knowledgeable individuals to get involved to ensure that policies are aligned with best practice. Advances in technology and research are likely to promote continuous improvement in statewide assessment programs (Haladyna, 2002). Because these policies are anticipated to have an important impact on teaching and learning, we encourage those with related expertise to seek out ways to be involved.

Participation Decision-Making Form for Students with Disabilities

Is this student also an English language learner (ELL)? _____. If yes, complete this form, and then complete the Participation Decision-Making Form for English language learners (Appendix 2.2).

It may be helpful to attach the following to this form, and provide copies to team members:

- a copy of the grade-level content, achievement, modified, and alternate achievement standards
- information on the testing format for the regular assessment and alternate assessment
- list of accommodations considered standard in your state
- information on any consequences associated with test participation (e.g., not eligible for merit awards, standard diploma, etc.)
- an accommodation form to be completed

Student name: _____   Date of birth: _____   Grade: _____

School: _____   Date form completed: _____

Team members participating (their role): _____

_____

_____

Checklist:

__ All team members have an understanding of the purpose of the accountability assessment

__ All team members have examined the content standards and grade-level achievement standards

__ All team members are familiar with the format of the regular assessment

__ All team members are aware of consequences associated with having the student participate under nonstandard conditions or on an alternate assessment

Brief statement/example of how student is accessing instruction in the content standards: _____

_____

_____

_____

_____

_____

_____

_____

(continued)

High achievement standards selected: *Mark one box for each content area. For any "modified" or "alternate" standards selected, provide brief explanation.*

Content area	Grade level	Modified*	Alternate	Explanation for modified or alternate standards
Math				
English/language arts				
Social studies				
Science				

*If modified is marked, explain here how standards are being modified: _____

_____

_____

_____

_____

Measurement strategy:

For all content areas above that are marked alternate, plan to administer an alternate assessment toward alternate achievement standards. Examine this alternate assessment format to determine whether accommodations may be needed for the student to access the test. If the student is an English language learner (ELL), complete the ELL participation decision-making form (Appendix 2.2). For all students with disabilities, use additional accommodation form to further determine how the student will participate [see Chapter 3].

For all content areas above that are marked modified, plan to administer alternate assessment toward modified standards. Examine the alternate assessment format to determine whether accommodations may be needed for the student to access the test. If the student is an English language learner (ELL), complete the ELL participation decision-making form (Appendix 2.2). For all students with disabilities, use additional accommodation form to further determine how the student will participate [see Chapter 3].

For each content area above that is marked "grade level," plan to administer the regular assessment. Examine the regular assessment format to determine whether accommodations may be needed for the student to access the test. If the student is an English language learner (ELL), also complete the ELL participation decision-making form (Appendix 2.2). For all students with disabilities, use additional accommodation form to further determine how the student will participate [see Chapter 3].

Participation Decision-Making Form
for English Language Learners

Is this student also a student with a disability? ___ If yes, complete the Participation Decision-Making Form for Students with Disabilities (Appendix 2.1), and then return to complete this form, along with the Accommodation Decision-Making Form for Students with Disabilities (Appendix 3.3).

It may be helpful to attach the following to this form, and provide copies to team members:

- a copy of the grade-level content and achievement standards for your state
- list of accommodations considered standard in your state
- information on any consequences associated with test participation (e.g., student not cligible for merit awards, standard diploma, etc.)

Student name: _____ Date of birth: _____ Grade: _____

School: _____ Date form completed: _____

No. of years that the student will have been enrolled in a U.S. school by testing day: _____

Team members participating (their role): _____

_____

_____

Checklist

__ All team members have an understanding of the purpose of the accountability assessment

__ All team members have examined the content standards and grade-level achievement standards

__ All team members are familiar with the format of the regular assessment

__ All team members are aware of consequences associated with having the student participate under nonstandard conditions

__ All team members know that the student will participate in an English Language Proficiency Test

How is the student currently instructed? (mark an "X")

Content area	English	Other language	Combination
Math			
English/language arts			
Social studies			
Science			

(continued)

How has the student been instructed in the past, and for how long? (mark years in boxes)

Content area	English	Other language	Combination
Math			
English/language arts			
Social studies			
Science			

Considering what you have provided in the tables above, which should be the focus of presentation of the regular assessment for this student?

Content area	English	Other language	Combination
Math			
English/language arts			
Social studies			
Science			

Note. English/language arts must be administered in English if the student has been enrolled in a public school for more than one year.

If other language of combination was marked, what specific other language accommodations will be used? (see accommodation attachment for standard accommodations)

_____

_____

_____

_____

What additional accommodations will be needed for the student to perform well according to the selected language of presentation? (see accommodation attachment for standard accommodations)

_____

_____

_____

_____

(continued)

Has the student used these accommodations before?   Yes No*

*If "no" was indicated above, what is the plan for familiarizing the student with these accommodations?

_____

_____

_____

_____

Is training needed for individuals to help with providing accommodations (e.g., a reader, a scribe)?   __ yes __ no

If yes, who will oversee this training? _____

Who will be responsible for ensuring that these accommodations are available to the student on the day of testing? _____

Note. If the ELL is also a student with a disability, also fill out Accommodation Decision-Making Form for Students with Disabilities (Appendix 3.3).

3

Testing Accommodations
for Students with Disabilities

Students with disabilities often have unique characteristics that make it difficult for them to demonstrate what they know and can do on standardized tests. For a long time, many students with disabilities were excluded from statewide testing in part because it was believed that the tests were not appropriate for them and also because there was a lack of flexibility in how tests could be administered. As accommodations have become more frequently allowed, participation rates of students with disabilities have increased (Olson & Goldstein, 1996). The provision of appropriate accommodations for students to participate in large-scale assessment programs is now mandated (IDEA, 1997). It is anticipated that nearly 70% of students with disabilities will be able to participate in the regular assessment used within an accountability system either with or without accommodations. When tests are designed from the beginning to be accessible to the widest variety of students, it is more likely that students with disabilities will be able to meaningfully participate. This concept of *universal design for assessment* is more fully described in Chapter 7. However, even when tests are developed using principles of universal design, some students with unique characteristics are likely to continue to have difficulties accessing the test. In the current chapter, we focus on methods for determining whether certain test alterations are appropriate in those situations in which such changes may be needed for the student to demonstrate their knowledge and skill on tests.

WHAT IS AN ACCOMMODATION?: THE IMPORTANCE
OF DEFINING TARGET SKILLS

Traditionally, there has been a reluctance to make changes in how standardized tests are administered. Standardized conditions are typically developed to ensure that the test measures similarly across all individuals (Anastasi, 1988). If changes are made in how the test is administered to certain individuals, there is a possibility that the test may become substantially easier for those particular students than for others who don't have access to the test change or that the test no longer measures what it is intended to measure. However, it is important to note that characteristics of the standardized testing conditions may make it particularly problematic for students with disabilities to show what they know and can do, thereby putting them at a specific disadvantage on the test. For example, it will be impossible for a student who is blind to demonstrate knowledge and skill on a test that is only presented in printed format. It may therefore be important for an accommodation to be made to allow the student to participate. This is often referred to as "leveling the playing field" through provision of an accommodation.

The example above (i.e., accommodating students who are blind on a test) may seem to be pretty clear-cut. It may not necessarily always be so clear. In fact, even in the example provided above, more information should have been provided to help in determining whether an accommodation is appropriate. What if the test was intended to be used in making a decision as to whether the person had the vision skills necessary to be a pilot? This test change would likely be considered much less appropriate if the test was (at least in part) intended to measure vision than if it was intended to measure something like social studies knowledge. Furthermore, the appropriateness of the accommodation may depend on whether the accommodation is likely to be available to the individual in the circumstances that the test is intended to predict. For example, it may be the case (in the far distant future!) that piloting becomes much more automatic and that flight navigation requires less accurate vision and much more accurate communication skills with those at airports. An accommodation for a blind individual on a pilot's test might actually be considered appropriate many years in the future!

IMPORTANT TERM DISTINCTIONS

There are a variety of terms that are often used when discussing changes in test administration conditions. In order to communicate well about the effectiveness of certain test changes, it is helpful to know some of the distinctions between these terms. Some terms that are used often refer to test changes in general, regardless of whether the change alters the construct intended to be measured by the test. These include terms such as *test alteration* and *test adaptation*. Other terms are often reserved for changes that result in a significant change in what is being measured compared to what is measured among other students. These include terms like *nonstandard accommodation* and *modification*. Finally, the terms *accommodation* or *standard accommodation* are often reserved for those test changes that are believed to maintain the integrity of the test (i.e., result in measurement of skills intended to be measured by the test).

It is very important to recognize how categorization of a test change as either an accommodation or modification depends on what the test is intended to measure. For example, if a math problem-solving test is intended to include measurement of fact knowledge, then allowing calculators on the test may lower the standard or expectation, and be considered a modification or nonstandard accommodation. However, if problem-solving skills are intended to be the focus of measurement, regardless of how the student gets to the answer (even if using a calculator), then the very same change of allowing a calculator might be considered an accommodation. Some additional examples of test changes that might be considered accommodations and modifications, depending on the intent of the test, are provided in Table 3.1.

To demonstrate knowledge and skill within a particular domain, students often need certain prerequisite skills. When students don't have the prerequisite skills, the test may not actually measure the intended domain. For example, calculation skills are a prerequisite skill that can interfere with measurement of math problem-solving skills on a test. For those with good calculation skills, a particular math test might be much more a measure of their math problem-solving skills than their calculation skills. For those with poor calculation skills, the test may not accurately represent their problem-solving skills because the lack of prerequisite skills hinders their ability to demonstrate problem-solving skills. Those who plan to use the test results to make decisions need to therefore decide whether such prerequisite skills are important to the skills that are intended to be measured on the test. In some cases, test users may consider calculation skills highly relevant. In other cases, test users may not consider them relevant and therefore consider use of a calculator as entirely appropriate.

It may be that certain items on a test are intended to measure such prerequisite skills, and other items are intended to measure higher-level skills. In these cases, it may be possible to make certain related accommodations available on certain items but not on others. For example, a calculator might be made available to students on items that are intended to measure math problem-solving skills, but not on items that are intended to measure math fact fluency. This can help to ensure that the test allows students to demonstrate their knowledge and skill in all areas that are intended to be tested. Another example of this is in

TABLE 3.1. **Classifications of Various Test Changes as Accommodations or Modifications**

Test change	Test change description	Situation in which it might be considered a modification	Situation in which it might be considered an accommodation
1. Read-aloud accommodation	Having someone (or something, such as a computer) read the test directions, items, and responses aloud to the student	Items/tests are intended to include measurement of the ability to decode	Items/tests are intended to measure ability to distinguish between various types of literature
2. Calculator	(self-explanatory)	Items/tests are intended to include measurement of fact knowledge	Items/tests are intended to include measurement of problem-solving skill alone
3. Dictated response	Having someone (or something, such as a tape recorder) record student responses	Items/tests are intended to measure writing skills	Items/tests are intended to measure content knowledge

language arts testing. In some cases, it may be the case that reading decoding skills are very important to measure, and so a read-aloud accommodation (i.e., having an assistant read aloud test item and content to the student) would not be considered appropriate. However, not ever providing this accommodation would make it impossible for students with severe decoding problems to demonstrate any English/language arts skills knowledge that they have developed apart from decoding skills. It therefore may make sense to allow a read-aloud accommodation on some of the items that are specifically intended to measure skills apart from decoding skills. However, before making decisions like this to provide various changes on part of a test, it is important for test users to decide exactly what the test is intended to measure, and more specifically, what each item is intended to measure. This can help determine whether an associated test change should be considered an accommodation or a modification.

IDENTIFYING UNIQUE STUDENT CHARACTERISTICS THAT INTERFERE WITH ACCURATE TEST MEASUREMENT

Although test developers aim to create tests that are accessible to the widest group of students, there are often characteristics of test formats and presentation that make it particularly difficult for certain groups of students to demonstrate their knowledge and skill. Tests are traditionally presented in a particular way that is accessible to a certain group of students, most commonly to those who have adequate vision and reading skills. Other aspects of how tests are administered may also cause specific difficulties for students with particular characteristics. For example, the requirement that students respond by completing a paper and pencil test may be particularly problematic for students who have difficulty manipulating a pencil. Some student characteristics that may make it particularly difficult to demonstrate knowledge and skill are described in the sections that follow.

Students with Sensory Challenges

Tests are often designed with the expectation that students will be able to view the items. However, this can create problems for the over 25, 000 students in U.S. schools who are either blind or who have limited vision. Some items may include very small print or may include the use of figures that are difficult for those with poor vision to discriminate. Furthermore, some figures may actually be very difficult for students with visual difficulties to understand, given the nature of their disability. Other testing difficulties frequently arise for the over 70,000 students in U.S. schools who have adequate sight, but are deaf or hard of hearing. These students are often slower in the development of reading skills (Lewis, 1996), given that the English language is sound based. Tests that involve substantial reading may therefore be difficult for students who have difficulties hearing.

Depending on the purpose of the test, it may or may not be reasonable to allow changes in test format to promote measurement of the intended skills and knowledge. For example, if the test is intended to determine whether the individual has adequate skills to become a pilot, it may not be appropriate to allow the individual to participate using a Braille edition, given that very good vision is needed to perform well as a pilot, and therefore is considered important to factor into decision making. However, if the test is intended to measure whether instruction is adding value to student outcomes, it would be highly inappropriate to make vision something that is tested, given that there is probably no way for instruction to affect a student's visual capabilities.

Some math problems with charts, graphs, and spatial estimation may be particularly difficult for students with visual problems (Bennett, Rock, & Novatkoski, 1989). Similarly, items that have a lot of text in them can be difficult for students who are deaf, given their difficulties in learning to read. In many situations, it may be possible to reduce the text of items and/or simplify charts, graphs, and figures to make them more accessible to people with associated difficulties. However, if understanding charts, graphs, and figures and decoding text are considered part of what is intended to be measured, it may not be appropriate to substantially alter these items.

Students with Physical Challenges

Tests are often designed such that students need to be able to manipulate a pen or pencil to show their skill and knowledge. This can be difficult for students who have significant physical or fine motor difficulties. Based on data available from the Office of Special Education Programs, over 60,000 students are receiving services for orthopedic impairments; many of these students may experience difficulties in taking a traditional standardized test. The need to demonstrate knowledge in the format of a paper-and-pencil test may prohibit students with such difficulties from demonstrating their knowledge, or it may slow them down and make it difficult for them to demonstrate the breadth and depth of their knowledge on a timed test. In circumstances in which a test is not intended to measure physical capabilities, an alternative format for the test may be necessary and appropriate.

Students with Specific Cognitive Challenges

Just as with students with sensory and physical difficulties, there may be aspects of how a test is administered that make it difficult for students with certain cognitive difficulties to demonstrate their knowledge and skill with respect to what is being measured. Well over three million students in the United States are receiving special education services due to an identified learning disability or mental impairment and may experience specific difficulties in demonstrating their knowledge under traditional testing conditions. Some students have trouble developing certain cognitive skills (e.g., reading skills) due to specific learning disabilities. Others have processing difficulties that make it such that they need extra time to read and understand information. These characteristics can conflict with tests that are presented in a format with heavy text, or those that are intended to be completed in a particular period of time. Again, if the test is not intended to measure these skills, it would only make sense to allow alternative formats for testing, or to relax the timing requirements to allow these students to participate.

Although making accommodations for students with physical and sensory difficulties has been considered appropriate, providing accommodations for students with cognitive difficulties has often been considered less appropriate (Bolt & Ysseldyke, 2008). This is likely due to the idea that cognitive skills are closely related to skills that are targeted for measurement. It is important to recognize that no matter whether the difficulty is considered physical or cognitive, it is most important to determine exactly what is intended to be measured by the test. This can allow individuals to make accommodation decisions that allow tests to more accurately predict student knowledge and skill across the domains that the test is intended to measure.

TYPES OF ACCOMMODATIONS

In 1993, the National Center on Educational Outcomes provided a categorization scheme for accommodations that is based on the general function the accommodation is intended to serve (Thurlow, Ysseldyke, & Silverstein, 1993). According to their scheme, students may need accommodations for the following reasons: (1) to facilitate effective *presentation* of test items, (2) to allow them to effectively *respond* to test items, (3) to allow them to participate according to a *schedule* that will help them best demonstrate their knowledge and skill, and/or (4) to participate in a *setting* that is conducive to their learning and demonstration of knowledge and skill. Accommodations that may be used for each of these functions are described in the sections that follow.

Presentation

Many test items are presented in ways that make it difficult for certain students to access them. For example, many test items are presented visually in a written format, which can limit students with poor vision and reading difficulties from demonstrating what they know with respect to what is intended to be measured. Presentation format can be altered in a variety of ways to facilitate student access to the test. Examples and associated research is described in the following sections.

Large Print

This accommodation may be helpful for students who have limited vision but can demonstrate adequate reading skills when text size is enhanced. A study published in the late 1980s indicated that this accommodation had relatively no effect on the construct being measured, suggesting that it was an appropriate change to make (Bennett, Rock, & Kaplan, 1987). Research has also investigated the extent to which this accommodation is helpful for students with learning disabilities, without clear support for providing it to this disability group alone (Brown, 1998; Burk, 1999; Fuchs, Fuchs, Eaton, Hamlett, Binkley, & Crouch, 2000). One of these studies suggested that in some circumstances, this accommodation may benefit all students, even those without disabilities (Brown, 1998).

Braille

This accommodation will likely only be helpful to those students who have learned Braille because of extremely limited or nonexistent vision. However, it is important to note that some items simply can not be translated into Braille, and therefore may be particularly difficult for students with visual impairments, regardless of whether a Braille version is made accessible to them. One study identified several types of items to be difficult for students taking a Braille version of the test (Bennett et al., 1987); however, overall, the test seemed to function similarly for students receiving this accommodation and other students taking the standard test. Items that appeared particularly difficult for those taking the Braille version over those involving graphs.

Read-Aloud

The read-aloud accommodation can take a variety of different forms. Most commonly, an assistant may read aloud the test directions, items, and responses to a student. In some cases, an audiotape recording may be created to standardize the process. With advances in technology, screen-reader programs are becoming more widely available to students with reading difficulties and can make it easier for students to access information and test content.

Having test content read aloud can be a very resource-intensive accommodation, particularly when it is provided on an individual basis. But it is something that many students may benefit from, given that tested material may be presented in a written format that is above their current reading level. Several studies have examined the helpfulness of this accommodation for students with learning disabilities. Some have found that this change differentially benefits students with learning disabilities (Tindal, Heath, Hollenbeck, Almond, & Harniss, 1998; Weston, 1999), others have found that it does not offer substantially greater benefits for students with disabilities (Kosciolek & Ysseldyke, 2000; McKevitt & Elliott, 2003; Meloy, Deville, & Frisbie, 2002; Schulte, Elliott, & Kratochwill, 2001), and still others have suggested that benefits of this accommodation depend on item type (Bolt & Thurlow, 2007; Fuchs, Fuchs, Eaton, Hamlett, & Karns, 2000). Understandably, when test items do not contain very much written text, the accommodation may not be necessary, but when there is substantial text, and the test is not intended to measure reading decoding skills, this accommodation may be appropriate for those who have difficulty decoding text.

A study of a video read-aloud accommodation and computer read-aloud accommodation among students with disabilities indicated that students tended to perform better under a student-paced computer read-aloud condition rather than a teacher-paced video read-aloud condition (Hollenbeck, Rozek-Tedesco, Tindal, & Glasgow, 2000). These results point to an important difference between how a student normally participates in testing and how his or her participation is altered when using certain types of read-aloud supports. Normally, students can easily skim, read, and reread sections of the test as they deem helpful. With a reader, audiotape, or video accommodation, it may be very challenging to do so. With screen-reading software, the normal testing experience that allows for skimming and rereading may be more accurately simulated. However, it is important for students to be familiar with whatever accommodation that they use prior to test administration; otherwise difficulties may arise in their use of the given accommodation. For instance, if a student is not familiar with screen-reading software, he or she may have difficulties making the program work, or difficulties making best use of the program during the administration of the test.

It is also important to recognize how provision of the read-aloud accommodation may necessitate the use of additional accommodations. For example, more time may be needed to read aloud test items given that speech can require more time than silent reading, and time may be needed for students to direct readers to reread portions that they would like to have reread. In addition, testing in an individual or small group setting may be needed to avoid distracting other students who do not need reading assistance. Testing individually with the read-aloud accommodation seems like it would be the best option, given that small group testing with the read-aloud accommodation may lead to students knowing and being influenced by how other students are responding (i.e., when the response choice "c" is read, several students bubble in their answer, suggesting that this is the correct answer, and perhaps influencing others to answer with this response, as well). Some guidelines for providing training to readers, as well as guidelines for other presentation accommodations can be found in a report published by the National Center on Educational Outcomes (see *www.education.umn.edu/NCEO/OnlinePubs/Synthesis58.html*).

Sign-Language Interpreter

This accommodation is one that is very frequently allowed in state accommodation policies (Bolt & Thurlow, 2004) and may be helpful for students who are deaf and hard of hearing, and know sign language. Given that students who are deaf may have difficulty learning to read, and given that reading is sound based, the provision of an interpreter may be helpful for many students who do not have adequate reading skills. In some states, such an accommodation may be standardized using a video of a sign-language interpretation. Although this can ensure that the interpreter does not accidentally "hint" at correct answers, or provide additional information that may lead students to the correct answer, it is important to recognize that there are many different variations of sign language, and it is important for the student to have access to the variation with which he or she is most familiar. Furthermore, it may be hard to translate certain words and phrases accurately into sign language; this could potentially be addressed when tests are developed to ensure that they will be accessible to all students. At this point, limited research was identified on the helpfulness of this accommodation, but given the reasons indicated above, it shows promise for being a helpful accommodation for certain students.

Response

Tests are often designed such that students need to know how to fill in bubbles or write extended responses to demonstrate their knowledge. Physical limitations or writing-skill deficits can make testing difficult for students. When a test is not intended to measure physical writing skills, it may be appropriate to provide some of the accommodations described below.

Proctor/Scribe

Just as students with reading difficulties may have difficulty accessing the content of test items, students with writing difficulties (whether due to motor or cognitive difficulties) may have trouble demonstrating their knowledge on a test. A proctor may be able to help a student mark his or her answers, or write down answers that the student provides to test items. Fuchs, Fuchs, Eaton, Hamlett, and Karns (2000) and Schulte et al. (2001) identified many students with disabilities who appeared to benefit substantially from this accommodation. However, other studies have suggested that this accommodation may lead to extremely high test scores that may not represent valid measurement of tested skills (Koretz, 1997; Trimble, 1998). It seems likely that without appropriate training, scribes may not be aware of the need to maintain a standardized way of recording student responses. Specific guidelines for provision of this accommodation are provided in a report from the National Center on Educational Outcomes (see *www.education.umn.edu/NCEO/OnlinePubs/Synthesis58.html*). It is important for scribes to be aware of what they can and can not add to student responses (e.g., correct spelling, punctuation, etc.). This will likely depend on the scope of what is intended to be measured on the particular test but should be determined in advance, with clear communication provided to assistants.

Computer/Machine

If students are adept at using a computer or word processor to answer questions and respond to instructional tasks, it seems appropriate to allow them to respond to test items in the same format. As access to technology increases, it may be the case that tests are actually administered to all students via computer. However, until this happens, it may be important to carefully consider and control how a computer response accommodation is provided. Recent research on this accommodation has suggested that it can be associated with more positive test results than paper-and-pencil formats, and that comparability of test construct can be maintained when a test is administered in this format (see Johnstone, Altman, Thurlow, & Thompson, 2006).

Writing in Test Booklets

Some students may get confused when attempting to transfer their response selections to an answer booklet and may benefit from being able to skip that extra step in the process of completing a test. It may be beneficial for them to simply mark their answers in a test booklet. Studies have suggested that this accommodation does not have a significant impact on the scores of students with disabilities (Rogers, 1983; Tindal et al., 1998; Tolfa-Veit & Scruggs, 1986). However, it is important to recognize that such studies often involve a large group of students with a variety of different disabilities, only some of whom may actually need the accommodation. Therefore, it may still be helpful for some students with disabilities.

Calculator

This accommodation is sometimes considered a presentation accommodation, and sometimes a response accommodation. In this chapter, we consider it a response accommodation, given that it is something that a student might choose to use when responding to a math item. This accommodation may be helpful in measuring certain math skills among students with computation difficulties. However, it is important for test developers and users to know exactly what skills they intend for the test to measure when deciding whether calculator use would be appropriate. Some tests allow a calculator to be used on certain items and not others that are intended to measure computation skill. Research has verified that certain items become extremely easy when calculators are allowed (Bridgeman, Harvey, & Braswell, 1995; Cohen & Kim, 1992; Loyd, 1991). However, other studies have shown that students with disabilities may benefit differentially from this accommodation on items designed to measure broader math problem-solving skills (Fuchs, Fuchs, Eaton, Hamlett, & Karns, 2000). In some cases, a calculator may be detrimental to solving math items if a student has not been trained how to appropriately use a calculator to find a particular answer. For example, identifying remainders for division problems using a calculator can be very difficult if one hasn't been taught a strategy for doing so. Similarly, fractions may be difficult to understand using certain calculators. In general, it seems very important for students to be familiar with the type of calculator that they will be using on the test in order to make the best use of it, and to be able to discriminate the items for which a calculator may be most useful.

Reinforcement for Task Completion

Some students may not be particularly motivated to participate in testing, and this lack of motivation may stem from a specific disability. In some cases, it may be appropriate to provide students incentives for completing items. It is important, however, to carefully control how this is done in order to make sure that a student puts forth his or her best effort. Correct responses typically can not be acknowledged during testing, and so students may only be able to receive reinforcement for task completion versus task accuracy. Unfortunately, this may lead students to rush through items rather than put forth their best effort. Even so, in some cases the provision of reinforcement might result in a better measure of their skills than not providing reinforcement. In some cases, there may exist substantial incentives for students to perform well, given that student-level consequences (e.g., graduation, grade promotion, etc.) are attached to the test score. In other cases, additional incentives may be helpful to engage certain students in the testing process. Elliott, Kratochwill, and McKevitt (2001) found that some students who received an accommodation package including reinforcement benefited substantially when the associated accommodations were provided. Additional studies have shown students with autism and preschoolers to score higher when incentives are provided (Blanding, Richards, Bradley-Johnson, & Johnson, 1994; Koegel, Koegel, & Smith, 1997; Willis & Shibata, 1978).

Scheduling

Statewide tests are often set up to be administered at a prespecified time and for a prespecified amount of time. Students with disabilities may need adjustments to these scheduling requirements if there are times during the day that they cannot perform optimally due to physical or mental limitations (e.g., chronic fatigue, need for medication to be at a particular threshold), or they may need a time extension or breaks between test sessions to allow for optimal performance. Some common scheduling accommodations are discussed below.

Extended Time

Due to physical limitations or mental processing limitations, some students may need extra time to complete tests. This is perhaps one of the more disputed accommodations, given that it is a change that has the possibility of benefiting *all* students when the test is timed. Research on the effectiveness of this accommodation for students with disabilities has indicated mixed support and nonsupport. A meta-analysis of extended time studies conducted in 1999 suggested that extended time has a very small differential effect on test scores for students with disabilities (Chiu & Pearson, 1999). Many believe that this accommodation is easy to provide and typically maintains the construct being measured (Gajria, Salend, & Hemrick, 1994; Jayanthi, Epstein, Polloway, & Bursuck, 1996). However, it is important to note that in some cases, the measurement of speed in completing tasks may be very important in determining competence. In these cases, extended time may not be an appropriate accommodation to provide. For scheduling purposes, it can be helpful to determine the amount of extended time to provide prior to test administration. Some other accommodations actually necessitate the use of extended time to ensure that they can be administered appropriately. For example, Braille typically takes longer to read than written material, and so additional time may be needed for students completing Braille test editions.

Test Breaks

In contrast to simply providing extended time, some students may benefit more from being able to take a break during testing. For some students, the demand to stay focused on a task for a long period of time may cause them to become very fatigued, and perform poorly toward the end of the test. A break from testing may help them refocus and perform consistently well throughout the test. However, it may be important to monitor students during breaks to ensure that they are not accessing specific information to help them correctly answer test items.

Setting

Typically, statewide tests are administered in a classroom setting to multiple groups of students at a time. However, this test environment may be problematic for certain students.

Students may be distracted by noises and commotion in a large class. Furthermore, they may be receiving accommodations that are distracting to other students in the class. In such circumstances, it may be important to allow the student to be monitored in taking the test in a separate setting, either individually, or with a small group of other students. Study carrels may also make it possible to minimize distractions for students who have difficulty concentrating.

IDENTIFYING THE BEST ACCOMMODATION PACKAGE

The accommodations described above are only a subset of the many accommodations that might be considered appropriate for students on statewide tests. Each student is different and has unique needs that may necessitate the use of unique accommodations. Determining what accommodations to provide to individual students requires much thought, and input from a variety of individuals, including the student, who tends to be the best informant on what changes may help facilitate meaningful test participation. Parents, teachers, individuals with knowledge of state standards and testing, and the individual student should be involved in making a team decision about what accommodations are necessary for appropriate participation. In making such decisions, they should take into consideration the state standards, characteristics of test presentation, response mode, scheduling, and setting, and unique characteristics of the individual student. They should also take into consideration the types of accommodations students have available to them during instruction. On tests that are intended to be used to predict performance in future environments, it is important to take into consideration the types of accommodations that may be easily accessed by the student in those future settings.

In 2005, collaborative work by individuals knowledgeable about state testing and accommodations, who were supported by the Council of Chief State School Officers, resulted in a document that provides guidance to states, districts, schools, and IEP teams as they go about making accommodation decisions (Thompson, Morse, Sharpe, & Hall, 2005). Within this document, they provide helpful tools to assist with decision making. One of these tools provides guidance to teams in answering questions about an individual student's needs. Answers to these questions can help in providing a link to potentially effective accommodations. This tool is provided in Appendix 3.1 of this chapter. Another very useful tool that the document includes is a checklist for ensuring that selected accommodations are actually implemented as intended on the day of the test. This tool is provided in Appendix 3.2 of this chapter. Research has suggested that what is documented for testing on a student's IEP is not always carried out (Shriner & DeStefano, 2003); it is important that there be checks and balances to ensure that accommodation plans are carried out.

Another tool that has been developed to assist with empirical determination of the accommodations that a student will benefit from is the Dynamic Assessment of Test Accommodations (DATA; Fuchs, Fuchs, Eaton, & Hamlett, 2002). Using this tool, a student completes minitests using a series of different testing accommodation packages to determine exactly which package results in the greatest benefit for the student. Although this may be a time-intensive process, it may provide the most accurate information on what accommodations are most appropriate for the student. However, decision makers must consider the results in light of whether the state standards are such that the accommodations would not artificially inflate the scores such that they no longer measure what it is considered important for them to measure.

When deciding what changes to allow during instruction, it is important to maintain a focus on accelerating student learning, and use this to guide whether a change is truly an appropriate change to make. It is very important to keep track of whether the student is actually *learning more* as a result of the change. Take, for example, the following scenario:

Ally is consistently failing her weekly spelling tests, spelling only 10 words out of 20 correct (50%) across 3 weeks. She is beginning to lose confidence in herself and is not motivated to study her spelling words like she did in the past when she was successful in learning them each week. Together, her parents, general education teacher, and special education teacher decide to reduce the number of spelling words that she has to learn each week to 12 in an attempt to increase her motivation, which they believe will ultimately lead to her learning more spelling words over time.

Suppose that over the course of the next 3 weeks, Ally earns 10 out of 12 correct (80%) on each of her spelling tests and feels slightly more confident in her spelling skills. Does this indicate that the accommodation in working to promote Ally's learning?

Although more time would perhaps be necessary to determine whether her skills would increase over time, at this point, Ally appears to be learning the same amount that she did prior to the change was put into place (i.e., 10 words per week). The change is therefore not necessarily promoting her learning, despite a higher score on the tests.

However, if Ally was earning 12/12 on her spelling tests, this might suggest that the change facilitated her learning, given that she was learning more with the change than without the change. Her parents and teacher may decide that it would be appropriate to increase the expectation over time, requiring her to learn more words over time.

In the initial scenario provided above, there was a clear lowering of expectations. For testing, this sort of change would not be considered an accommodation, but rather a modification because it lowers standards. However, it is important to recognize that in some cases, a lowering of standards may be necessary in instruction to facilitate learning. What is most important is to maintain a measurement scheme that will allow you to determine whether the modification is truly facilitating student learning. In this case, it was necessary for the team to monitor the number of words learned each week rather than the percent of total words correctly spelled in order to know whether the change was truly facilitating learning.

RECOGNIZING POTENTIAL DRAWBACKS OF ACCOMMODATIONS

Sometimes provision of an accommodation can lead to additional challenges to appropriate testing; it is important for these to be minimized as much as possible. Earlier, issues associated with providing reading assistance were discussed. Students who have the test read aloud may find it difficult to skim or to have certain sections reread in contrast to reading the test on their own. It therefore is important for students to have practice using this accommodation prior to testing, so that they know how to make best use of the accommodation. Providing a large-print accommodation may make it such that items are split across pages, requiring students to flip forward and back as they try to make sense out of an item. Sign-language interpretations may not be able to fully communicate the actual content of the test item with a high level of accuracy. Providing a scribe may become tedious if the student must spell out words and orally provide punctuation. Furthermore, certain students may be embarrassed to make use of certain accommodations, such as having to leave the room to take the test in a separate setting, or use a study carrel to minimize distractions. As a result, they may avoid using them. Decision makers should carefully consider all such potential ramifications of providing accommodations and seek to minimize any barriers to their effective use in testing.

INDIVIDUAL STUDENTS' ACCOMMODATION NEEDS WILL LIKELY CHANGE OVER TIME

Students' difficulties are rarely stagnant. The gap between their skills and the skills needed to effectively participate in grade-level testing and instruction may change over time. In fact, in many circumstances, the goal is for students to overcome the difficulties that originally make it such that they need accommodations, and so it is expected that their accommodation needs will change. For example, with effective reading remediation, students with reading difficulties may eventually reach the level of reading competence needed to participate in a statewide math test without needing an accommodation, or may be able to best participate with extended time to allow them to read the material on their own. In such circumstances, providing students with a read-aloud accommodation may actually interfere with effective testing. Therefore, it is important to regularly evaluate whether accommodations are meeting the needs of students. This should happen on an annual basis, at the very minimum. Students themselves can be very important informants for accommodation decision making. They often know better than anyone else what they do and don't need to access instruction, and what they need to perform optimally on a test.

STATE ACCOMMODATION POLICIES

As indicated in earlier sections of this chapter, it is first and foremost important to consider the student's unique needs in light of the skills and knowledge intended to be tested to determine what kinds of test changes might be needed to facilitate test access. However, many states have specific policies about what test changes can be considered standard or "okay" accommodations that maintain the integrity of the statewide test. Decisions about what accommodations can be considered "appropriate" are made at the state level, given that each state has a unique set of standards that students are expected to meet. Depending on the nature of those standards, the skills and knowledge intended to be tested may vary. In some cases, there may be certain limitations put on accommodation use. For example, a certain accommodation may only be allowed for certain portions of the test, or for certain test content areas. Or, it may be the case that a certain change may be provided, but that when provided, the test administration is then considered "nonstandard," and scores are not considered valid. Although it is important to consider potential ramifications of allowing students to participate in the test with certain test changes (e.g., student's test administration may not count toward meeting the graduation requirement given that it was administered with a nonstandard accommodation), it is most important to advocate that students receive the accommodations necessary for them to meaningfully participate in state testing. When an accommodation that is considered necessary for the student's skills to be effectively measured is not considered appropriate according to the state accommodation policy, it may be important to advocate for changes in policy, or for exceptions to be made in order for the student's unique needs to be addressed. IEP team members may want to contact the state department of education in order to suggest that such an exception be made. To find out more information on the accommodation policy in your state, go to *education.umn.edu/ nceo/TopicAreas/Accommodations/StatesAccomm.htm*, where you can find a link to your state's accommodation policy.

ALIGNING TESTING AND INSTRUCTIONAL ACCOMMODATIONS

The ultimate purpose of large-scale assessment and accountability systems is to promote the learning of all students toward prespecified standards. Accountability testing is intended to help in determining whether instruction is allowing students to meet the given standards. Instruction is anticipated to include the exact skills and knowledge that are tested. It follows that if an accommodation is considered necessary for the student to access instruction, the student will likely need it to access testing, and vice versa. If students fail to receive accommodations on a test that they received during instruction, they may not be able to demonstrate what they have actually learned. If students fail to receive accommodations during instruction, they may not be comfortable using the accommodation on the test. Worse yet, they may be denied access to instruction that might help them score higher on the test when accommodated. Some accommodations can be very resource intensive, and there may be a tendency to provide them when it "counts" (i.e., on the test), but not provide them as frequently during instruction. Unfortunately, this may hinder students from accessing useful instruction such that they *can* perform well on the test. A recent study suggested that the effects of a read-aloud accommodation for students with reading difficulties were particularly salient on easy math items that were considered difficult to read rather than on more difficult math items that were considered difficult to read (Bolt & Thurlow, 2007). One potential explanation for this finding is that students aren't able to access instruction in more difficult math concepts, which may be due to the existence of heavy reading loads in math instruction for which students are not receiving accommodations. Some additional studies have suggested that there may be a lack of alignment between what accommodations are indicated on students' IEPs and what is provided in class and during testing (Bottsford-Miller, Thurlow, Stout, & Quenemoen, 2006; Shriner & DeStefano, 2003).

In some cases, there may be very stringent rules about which accommodations are allowed on the statewide test. It is important to be aware of these rules, and to work toward having students accommodated during instruction in the same way that they will be accommodated in testing. However, in some cases it may make sense to be more flexible in providing instructional changes if the changes are considered necessary to promote the student's learning. It is up to those individuals closest to the student to determine what changes may best facilitate the student's learning toward standards.

ENSURING APPROPRIATE REMEDIATION WHILE PROVIDING ACCOMMODATIONS

One important concern that may arise when deciding to provide accommodations is that accommodation provision may result in a deemphasis on the need for intervention to address basic skill deficits. For instance, if a read-aloud accommodation is made available for a student to access instruction and testing across a variety of content areas, there may be less incentive for the student to actually learn to read; the accommodation may become a "crutch" that the student learns to depend on and cannot function without. It is therefore extremely important to continue to provide intervention despite making the decision to accommodate. This also highlights the importance of identifying exactly what skills and knowledge are targeted for students to learn. When this is clarified, it becomes much easier to determine whether an accommodation is becoming a "crutch" versus something that facilitates learning.

With advances in technology, new tools can often serve intervention and accommodation purposes and may ultimately promote student learning in very meaningful ways. For example, computer screen-reading programs not only accommodate students by giving them access to written material, but also can serve as a sort of intervention tool in which students can practice pairing sounds with words, given that the program highlights text as it simultaneously "reads" the text aloud. This may help facilitate students' skills in decoding and promote reading fluency. Making use of such a tool may be particularly helpful for students with reading difficulties.

PROMOTING STUDENT SELF-ADVOCACY SKILLS

A stigma unfortunately remains attached to disability status that is not likely to be eliminated in the near future. Many students, particularly those at the secondary level and beyond, may be embarrassed to ask for or make use of needed accommodations because of the stigma that is often attached to their disability status. Preliminary data from a survey of college students with reading difficulties who reported on their experiences with accommodations during high school suggests that students may be reluctant to ask for accommodations, given related embarrassment (Bolt & Decker, 2007). Furthermore, many students indicated having an easier time accessing accommodations in college than in high school.

Some college students indicated not being aware of accommodations that might have been available to them in high school.

Although all students should be familiar with what accommodations they need to access instruction and testing, it is particularly important that at the secondary level students are taught skills for ensuring that they will continue to have access to needed accommodations in their educational and employment environments following graduation. They need to know their rights, as well as appropriate methods for ensuring that their rights are not denied. Several researchers have highlighted the importance of teaching students how to advocate for their needs and have suggested that more of this needs to occur in school settings (Mason, Field, & Sawilowsky, 2004; Test, Fowler, Wood, Brewer, & Eddy, 2005). According to Test et al. (2005), students need to have adequate knowledge of themselves, knowledge of their rights, and effective communication and leadership skills. Having self-determination goals included as part of a student's IEP, and ensuring that students meaningfully participate in the development of their IEP, can help to promote a student's development of related skills.

EVALUATING ACCOMMODATION USE AND EFFECTIVENESS: SOME GUIDING QUESTIONS

It is extremely important to constantly evaluate the extent to which accommodations are helpful, and appropriate. The Council of Chief State School Officers' collaborative document mentioned earlier in this chapter provides some very nice tools to guide the evaluation process. Questions that they provide to guide evaluation at the district/school level, as well as at the individual student level, are presented in Figure 3.1.

THE CHANGING NATURE OF WHAT IS NEEDED FOR SUCCESS IN SOCIETY

The world is becoming a much more accessible place for people with disabilities. Because disability is defined by the extent to which an individual's capabilities deviate from societal expectations, which change over time, what constitutes a disability now may not constitute a disability in the future. As technology advances, accommodations can become much easier to provide and actually can become incorporated in everyday activities, making it less of a challenge for individuals to advocate for accommodation availability. For example, many students who are blind may have previously been denied access to certain occupations, given that it would be exceptionally difficult to translate material needed for the job into a Braille format. However, now it is possible for individuals who are blind to have nearly full access to information on the Internet using screen-reading programs. When making decisions about how to accommodate students with disabilities, it is important to recognize how technology may change the opportunities available to them in the future. Furthermore, students with disabilities should be encouraged to stay abreast of new technological advances that may help alleviate the difficulties that they current experience. Given the

QUESTIONS TO GUIDE EVALUATION OF ACCOMMODATION USE AT THE SCHOOL OR DISTRICT LEVEL

1. Are there policies to ensure ethical testing practices, the standardized administration of assessments, and that test security practices are followed before, during, and after the day of the test?
2. Are there procedures in place to ensure test administration procedures are not compromised with the provision of accomodations?
3. Are students receiving accommodations as documented in their IEP and 504 plans?
4. Are there procedures in place to ensure that test administrators adhere to directions for the implementation of accommodations?
5. How many students with IEPs or 504 plans are receiving accommodations?
6. What types of accommodations are provided and are some used more than others?
7. How well do students who receive accommodations perform on state and local assessments? If students are not meeting the expected level of performance, is it due to the students not having had access to the necessary instruction, not receiving the accommodation, or using the accommodations that were not effective?

QUESTIONS TO GUIDE EVALUATION AT THE STUDENT LEVEL

1. What accommodations are used by the student during instruction and assessments?
2. What are the results of classroom assignments and assessments when accommodations are used versus when accommodations are not used? If a student did not meet the expected level of performance, is it due to not having access to the necessary instruction, not receiving the accommodations, or using accommodations was ineffective?
3. What is the student's perception of how well the accommodation worked?
4. What combinations of accommodations seem to be effective?
5. What are the difficulties encountered in the use of accommodations?
6. What are the perceptions of teachers and others about how the accommodation appears to be working?

FIGURE 3.1. Questions to guide evaluation of accommodation use. From Thompson, Morse, Sharpe, and Hall (2005). Copyright 2005 by the Council of Chief State School Officers. *Accommodations Manual: How to Select, Administer, and Evaluate Use of Accommodations for Instruction and Asessment of Students with Disabilities.* Washington, DC: Author. *www.ccsso. org/projects/scass/projects/assessing_special_education_students/11302.cfm.* Reprinted by permission.

ever-changing nature of technology, and the skills needed to be successful in society, it is important to maintain high expectations and support students in developing high-level thinking skills, given that any basic skill deficits may be very easily addressed by technological advances in the future.

CASE EXAMPLE (CONTINUED): ROBERT

In Chapter 2, we provided information about how participation decisions were made for a student named Robert. In this section, we continue this case and describe how accommodation decisions were made for Robert.

Robert is a third-grade student with severe autism. He has extreme difficulties in completing work independently. He currently receives 1:1 assistance in each of his classes to ensure implementation of a comprehensive behavior management plan and appropriate training in independent functioning. He is very inconsistent in demonstrating knowledge and skill in academic areas. On some class assignments, he scores 100%, and on others, he scores 0%. This is true across content areas. He tends to be stronger in math than in English language arts. He has been observed to read out loud with fluency on occasion. The team decided that Robert should participate in the regular assessment with accommodations (see example description in Chapter 2). Follow along with Figure 3.2 to understand how the team made decisions about how Robert would be accommodated. A blank version of the Accommodation Decision-Making Form for Students with Disabilities is presented in Appendix 3.3.

Accommodation Decision-Making Form for Students with Disabilities
(Can be attached to the participation form
Decision-Making for Students with Disabilities [Appendix 2.1])

Student name: <u>Robert Jones</u>　　　　Date of birth: <u>October 5, 1999</u>　　Grade: <u>3</u>

School: <u>Jefferson Elementary</u>　　　　Date form completed: <u>January 9, 2008</u>

Team members participating (their role): <u>Susan and Brian Jones (Robert's parents), Anita Jacobs (Robert's 1:1</u>

<u>assistant), John Smith (general education teacher), Roberta Johnson (special education teacher),</u>

<u>Joel Oosterhouse (principal)</u>

This student will participate in the:

X Regular assessment

__ Alternate assessment-grade-level standards

__ Alternate assessment-modified standards

__ Alternate assessment-alternate standards

Examine information on the <u>format of</u> the test in which the student will participate.
What skills unrelated to what the test is measuring are needed for the student to demonstrate skill and knowledge in which he or she may be deficient? *(e.g., manipulate a pencil, decode printed material, etc.).*

1.　An adequate independent level of functioning to complete paper-and-pencil tasks

2.　Completing activities without external reinforcement

3.　Internal cues to remember to check over work

4.

5.

6.

How is the student accommodated for these problems during instruction?

1.　Behavior plan implemented by 1:1 assistant

2.　Reinforcement provided every 20 minutes

3.　Visual cues to remind him to check over work

4.

5.

6.

(add more on back as needed)

Of these accommodations, which are considered "standard" according to state policy?

1.　Visual cues

2.　Reinforcement at periodic intervals

3.

4.

5.

6.

(add more as needed)

(continued)

FIGURE 3.2. Completed example for Robert of the Accommodation Decision-Making Form for Students with Disabilities.

Which accommodations will be provided on the test? Note: If any accommodations are selected that are not standard, and the team thinks allow for better measurement for the given student, the team should contact the state department to advocate for their use.

1.   *Implementation of behavior management plan**

2.   *Visual cues to support in checking over work*

3.   *Reinforcement at periodic intervals*

4.

5.

6.

nonstandard—will contact state department for how to report

Is the student familiar with using these accommodations?   X yes   __ no

If no, what will be done to familiarize the student with these accommodations?

Is training needed for individuals to help with providing accommodations (e.g., a reader, a scribe)?
                                          X yes   __ no

(to ensure that the 1:1 assistant knows to not help him in completing the test)

If yes, who will oversee this training? *Assessment program coordinator from the district*

Who will be responsible for ensuring that these accommodations are available to the student on the day of testing? *1:1 assistant, district assessment program coordinator*

FIGURE 3.2. *(continued)*

Access Needs That May Require Accommodations

Directions: Use these questions to identify various types of presentation, response, setting, and timing and scheduling accommodations for students with disabilities. The list is not exhaustive— its purpose is to prompt members of IEP teams and 504 planning committees to consider a wide range of accommodation needs. Use the list in planning by indicating Y (YES), N (NO), or DK/NA (Don't Know or Not Applicable).

	Y	N	DK/NA
PRESENTATION ACCOMMODATIONS			
1. Does the student have a visual impairment that requires large-type or Braille materials?	☐	☐	☐
2. Is the student able to read and understand directions?	☐	☐	☐
3. Can the stundent follow oral directions from an adult or audiotape?	☐	☐	☐
4. Does the student need directions repeated frequently?	☐	☐	☐
5. Are assistive technology devices indicated on the student's IEP?	☐	☐	☐
6. Has the student been identified as having a reading disability?	☐	☐	☐
7. Does the student have low or poor reading skills that may require the reading of tests or sections of tests that do not measure reading comprehension in order to demonstrate knowledge of subject areas?	☐	☐	☐
8. Does the student have a hearing impairment that requires an interpreter to sign directions?	☐	☐	☐
9. Does the student have a hearing impairment and need a listening device?	☐	☐	☐
RESPONSE ACCOMMODATIONS			
10. Does the student have difficulty tracking from one page to another and maintaining that student's place?	☐	☐	☐
11. Does the student have a disability that affects the ability to record that student's responses in the standard manner?	☐	☐	☐
12. Can the student use a pencil or writing instrument?	☐	☐	☐
13. Does the student use a word processor to complete homework assignments or tests?	☐	☐	☐
14. Does the student use a tape recorder to complete assignments or tests?	☐	☐	☐
15. Does the student need the services of a scribe?	☐	☐	☐
16. Does the student have a disability that affects that student's ability to spell?	☐	☐	☐
17. Does the student have a visual or motor disability that affects that student's ability to perform math computations?	☐	☐	☐

(continued)

	Y	N	DK/ NA

SETTING ACCOMMODATIONS

18. Do others easily distract the student or does that student have difficulty remaining on task? ☐ ☐ ☐

19. Does the student require any specialized equipment or other accommodations that may be distracting to others? ☐ ☐ ☐

20. Does the student have visual or auditory impairments that require special lighting or acoustics? ☐ ☐ ☐

21. Can the student focus on the student's own work in a setting with large groups of other students? ☐ ☐ ☐

22. Does the student exhibit behaviors that may disrupt the attention of other students? ☐ ☐ ☐

23. Do any physical accommodations need to be made for the student in the classroom? ☐ ☐ ☐

TIMING AND SCHEDULING ACCOMMODATIONS

24. Can the student work continuously for the length of time allocated for standard test administration? ☐ ☐ ☐

25. Does the student use other accommodations or adaptive equipment that require more time to complete test items (e.g., Braille, scribe, use of head pointer to type)? ☐ ☐ ☐

26. Does the student tire easily due to health impairments? ☐ ☐ ☐

27. Does the student have a visual impairment that causes eyestrain and requires frequent breaks? ☐ ☐ ☐

28. Does the student have a learning disability that affects the rate at which that student processes written information? ☐ ☐ ☐

29. Does the student have a motor disability that affects the rate at which that student writes responses? ☐ ☐ ☐

30. Does tile student take any type of medication to facilitate optimal performance? ☐ ☐ ☐

31. Does the student's attention span or distractibility require shorter working periods and frequent breaks? ☐ ☐ ☐

APPENDIX 3.2

Logistics Planning Checklist

Directions: This Logistics Planning Checklist can be used in the planning and implementation of assessment accommodations for an individual student. Use the checklist by indicating Y (Yes), N (No), or NA (Not Applicable).

	Y	N	NA
ACCOMMODATIONS THROUGHOUT THE ACADEMIC YEAR			
1. Accommodations are documented on student's IEP or 504 plan.	☐	☐	☐
2. Student uses accommodations regularly and evaluates use.	☐	☐	☐
3. A master accommodations plan/data base listing assessment accommodation needs for all students tested is updated regularly.	☐	☐	☐
PREPARATION FOR TEST DAY			
4. Special test: editions are ordered for individual students based on information contained in master accommodations plan (e.g., audio tape, Braille, large print).	☐	☐	☐
5. Test administrators/proctors receive a list of accommodation needs for students they will supervise (list comes from master accommodations plan/ data base).	☐	☐	☐
6. Adult supervision is arranged and test administrators receive training for each student receiving accommodations in small group or individual settings, including extended time (with substitutes available).	☐	☐	☐
7. Trained readers, scribes, and sign language interpreters are arranged for individual students (with substitutes available).	☐	☐	☐
8. Special equipment is arranged and checked for correct operation (e.g., calculator, tape recorder, word processor).	☐	☐	☐
ACCOMMODATIONS ON THE DAY OF THE TEST			
9. All eligible students receive accommodations as determined by their IEP or 504 plan.	☐	☐	☐
10. Provision of accommodations is recorded by test administrator.	☐	☐	☐
11. Substitute providers of accommodations are available as needed (e.g., interpreters, readers, scribes)	☐	☐	☐
12. Plans are made to replace defective equipment.	☐	☐	☐
CONSIDERATION AFTER THE DAY OF THE TEST			
13. Responses are transferred to scannable answer sheets for students using special equipment and adapted test forms and response documents.	☐	☐	☐
14. All equipment is returned to appropriate locations.	☐	☐	☐
15. Students who take make-up tests receive needed accommodations.	☐	☐	☐
16. Effectiveness of accommodations use is evaluated by test administrators and students, and plans are made for improvement.	☐	☐	☐

From Thompson, Morse, Sharpe, and Hall (2005). Copyright 2005 by the Council of Chief State School Officers. *Accommodations Manual: How to Select, Administer, and Evaluate Use of Accommodations for Instruction and Asessment of Students with Disabilities.* Washington, DC: Author. *www.ccsso.org/projects/scass/projects/assessing_special_education_students/11302.cfm*. Reprinted by permission.

Accommodation Decision-Making Form for Students with Disabilities

(Can be attached to the Participation Decision-Making Form for Students with Disabilities [Appendix 2.1])

Student name: _____   Date of birth: _____   Grade: _____

School: _____   Date form completed: _____

Team members participating (their role): _____

_____

_____

This student will participate in the:

__ Regular assessment

__ Alternate assessment-grade-level standards

__ Alternate assessment-modified standards

__ Alternate assessment-alternate standards

Examine information on the format of the test in which the student will participate.
What skills unrelated to what the test is measuring are needed for the student to demonstrate skill and knowledge in which he or she may be deficient? *(e.g., manipulate a pencil, decode printed material, etc.).*

1.

2.

3.

4.

5.

6.

How is the student accommodated for these problems during instruction?

1.

2.

3.

4.

5.

6.

(add more on back as needed)

(continued)

Of these accommodations, which are considered "standard" according to state policy?

1.

2.

3.

4.

5.

6.

(add more as needed)

Which accommodations will be provided on the test? Note: If any accommodations are selected that are not standard, and the team thinks allow for better measurement for the given student, the team should contact the state department to advocate for their use.

1.

2.

3.

4.

5.

6.

Is the student familiar with using these accommodations? ___ yes ___ no

If no, what will be done to familiarize the student with these accommodations?

Is training needed for individuals to help with providing accommodations (e.g., a reader, a scribe)? ___ yes ___ no

If yes, who will oversee this training? _____

Who will be responsible for ensuring that these accommodations are available to the student on the day of testing? _____

4

Testing Accommodations
for English Language Learners

The number of students attending U.S. public schools who are not proficient in English is increasing at a very rapid rate. As of 2000, one-fifth of pre–K to 12th-grade students were children of immigrants (Capps et al., 2005). In addition, the number of native language backgrounds represented in U.S. public schools is well over 300, and the number of students from non-English language backgrounds is expected to increase in the coming decades (National Center for Education Statistics, 2004). NCLB requires that states develop standards for English language proficiency and evaluate the progress of ELLs toward those standards. In addition, large-scale assessment and accountability systems that are developed to measure the academic skills and knowledge for the general population also need to include ELLs. In fact, ELLs are often a separate subgroup for which AYP must be evident over time in order for educational agencies to avoid certain sanctions and consequences. However, the tests associated with these broad academic skill and knowledge assessment programs are developed in English and have been shown to have poor reliability and validity for students with limited English proficiency (Abedi, Leon, & Mirocha, 2003). Although issues associated with the development of appropriate English language proficiency assessments are important to address, we focus our attention in this chapter on how to make broader academic skill and knowledge assessment programs more accessible to ELLs.

How can we promote valid assessment for students from different language backgrounds who are still learning the English language? When does it make sense to provide a native language accommodation to such students, and when might it be important for them to participate in testing in English? In this chapter, we discuss (1) ELL characteristics that are important for deciding how to accommodate individual ELLs in large-scale assessment programs, (2) common ELL testing accommodations and the research available to support their use, and (3) procedures to follow to ensure each ELL is provided appropriate accommodations.

WHAT IS AN ACCOMMODATION?: IDENTIFYING TARGET SKILLS FOR ELLS

As is the case for determining appropriate accommodations for student with disabilities, it is very important to clarify what the target skills and knowledge for an assessment are prior to making accommodation decisions for ELLs. In some circumstances, competence in the English language is part of what is intended to be tested, and so providing accommodations to address limited English proficiency would not be appropriate (Phillips, 2002). In other circumstances, the goal of testing is to determine whether the student has developed skills and knowledge in an area, regardless of the language(s) in which he or she can perform the given tasks. It is very important for state and local educational agencies to carefully determine the assessment areas in which performance within the English language is considered essential to showing proficiency in the targeted domain. English/language arts is an area in which test performance in (and proficiency with) English is typically necessary. However, if some of the state standards to be measured include skills that apply in other languages, then state and district policymakers should make it clear whether performance in a non-English language could be considered to meet the standards.

Once guidance has been provided as to whether performance in English is essential, the decision-making team knows which assessment areas can possibly be addressed using a different language for presentation. However, deciding the language in which the test material should be presented, and the accommodations that should be provided for individual students remains a challenging task. This is particularly true given that there are a variety of instructional and individual student variables that may affect the language in which the student is likely to demonstrate optimal performance.

CONSIDERING UNIQUE STUDENT CHARACTERISTICS

Prior Academic Experiences

ELLs come from a variety of different backgrounds. Some have lived in the United States since they were born and have only experienced academic instruction in the United States. Others move to the United States during their teenage years and have had substantial academic instruction in their native country. Others may move in their teenage years and have no prior schooling. In order to determine how students should participate, it is important to know whether they may have been exposed to learning the same skills in their native language sometime in the past. If they have received instruction in their native language, it may be easier for them to translate this learning into a new language (Collier, 1987). If they have, it may be appropriate to have them tested with a native language accommodation. However, this should be considered in light of other individual and instructional characteristics when deciding how to best accommodate ELLs.

Current Academic Experiences

There are several variations in how schools provide instruction to ELLs. Bilingual instruction, English immersion, and sheltered English instruction are just some of the ways in which students may be taught academic skills in U.S. schools. Depending on how they are being taught, it may make more sense for them to be tested in English versus in their native language. In bilingual classrooms, the goal is for students to become proficient in both languages. If they happen to be more proficient in one language than in another, it may make more sense to offer the test to them in the language of greater proficiency. However, it is important to recognize that simply being "more proficient" in one language than in another does not necessarily mean that they have adequate language proficiency to optimally show what they know and can do on a particular test in that language. If English immersion is the strategy used for instruction, it may make more sense to test in English because this may be the only language in which the student has been exposed to the tested concepts. The way in which instruction is provided should be taken into consideration along with the information on the students' prior academic learning experiences to make accommodation decisions. For example, if a student has only been in an English immersion program for a short time and has a lot of prior academic learning experience from his or her native country, it may be more reasonable to provide a native language accommodation than to test in English.

At the same time, it is important that the instructional approach that is used to teach ELLs academic skills (e.g., sheltered English, English immersion, bilingual programming, etc.) promotes optimal learning toward the state standards. If the state standards are heavily focused on student demonstration of academic proficiency in English, then it may be particularly important for the school to provide instruction using a strategy that will best facilitate that goal, with less emphasis on facilitating learning in the student's native language. Therefore, although consideration should be given to the instructional approach used, the state standards should be the ultimate guide for what native language accommodations should be considered appropriate. If the state standards are not language specific, then the instructional approach being used should be taken into consideration to determine the types of accommodations that might be most effective for the individual student.

Variables Associated with Second-Language Development

Not only is it important to take into consideration prior academic learning and current instruction, but it is also important to recognize more general language development patterns in order to inform accommodation decision making. In all cases, accommodation decisions should be made on an individual student basis; given the complexities associated with language acquisition, this seems particularly important.

Cummins (1984) posited a theory of language acquisition that describes two primary types of language: basic interpersonal communication skills (BICS) and cognitive academic language proficiency (CALP). BICS take comparatively little time to develop; they are the language skills most commonly associated with everyday conversation. However, CALP typically takes much longer to develop and represents the skills needed for academic learning in a new language. When students have developed CALP in their native language, it is believed that they can translate this into CALP in English much faster than if they have not yet developed CALP in their native language. When considering this information in light of making accommodation decisions, the student may need to have developed CALP in English to truly be able to perform optimally on a given test. Depending on prior academic learning, and the amount of time that the student has been in the United States, he or she may not have developed CALP in English. When this is the case, it may be necessary to find ways to accommodate the student during testing. This would not necessarily take the form of a native language accommodation, particularly if the student has not been taught the tested skills in his or her native language; however, it may mean that the student would benefit from extra time or a dictionary accommodation when those are allowed as a part of statewide testing.

In addition, it is important to recognize that English language development among ELLs may be affected by their level or pattern of acculturation, which refers to the way in which individuals from different cultures adapt when coming into continuous contact with one another (Redfield, Linton, & Herskovits, 1936). Acculturation may be related to a variety of different factors, such as the nature and intensity of contact between the two cultures, the strategies the student has for acculturating, the political context, as well as many other factors (Berry, Poortinga, Segall, & Dasen, 2002). Opportunities for language development may be related to the extent to which a child's family is connected to others who speak English, as well as the degree to which they desire to become part of the new culture. Therefore, it is important to not use time alone to mark where a student should be in terms of English language development; one must consider time in the context of many other individual and community factors that may play a role.

TYPES OF ACCOMMODATIONS

Although some accommodations that are commonly considered for students with disabilities may also apply to ELLs, accommodations that are intended to reduce linguistic difficulties or barriers associated with testing are typically the focus of discussion for this population. The National Center on Educational Outcomes has categorized accommodations for ELLs in terms of how they affect the language that is used to convey test content and the language in which students respond to test items. The categories include native language, English language, and nonlinguistic accommodations. When compared to accommodations for students with disabilities, fewer research studies currently exist on the impact of accommodations for ELLs. However, several recent reviews of the existing research in this area have been conducted (Abedi, Hofstetter, & Lord, 2004; Francis, Rivera, Lesaux, Kieffer, & Rivera, 2006; Wolf et al., 2008); readers are encouraged to examine these reviews in greater detail for more information on this topic. Specific accommodations associated with each of the accommodation types (i.e., native language, English language, and nonlinguistic accommodations) are described in the following sections, along with a summary of any related research that has been reviewed.

Native Language Accommodations

Perhaps one of the most instinctive accommodations to consider for an ELL is allowing the student to take a test in his or her native language. Although this may be an appropriate accommodation for some ELLs, it is very important to recognize the many limitations and drawbacks of this approach, and how these accommodations may not represent the best option for helping students demonstrate their skill and knowledge for a variety of reasons. Given the many different languages represented among students in U.S. schools today, making these kinds of accommodations available can be very resource intensive. It is clearly necessary to examine the extent to which these types of accommodations are effective before spending a large amount of money and time on developing native language translations and identifying individuals who can help with oral translations of test items.

Direct Word-for-Word Translations

A substantial amount of research has been conducted that identifies many issues associated with translating test items (Hambleton & Patsula, 1998; Sireci, 1997; Sireci, Yang, Harter, & Ehrlich, 2006). In some cases, there may be no easy translation of English language words into other languages. The most common and accepted method for creating test translations involves back translation, in which a test is translated into a new language by one person, and another individual then takes the translated test and translates it back into English. The original English version and "back-translated" version are then compared. When the back translation does not appropriately match the original version, more work is needed to create an appropriate translation. Duran, Brown, and McCall (2002) describe a process that was used in Oregon to create Spanish–English assessments, which involved the establishment of a "Bilingual Review Panel" that carefully reviewed the translation of various items on the statewide math test.

Perhaps more important, a translated test version will be of limited use to a student if he or she has only been exposed to the concepts tested in English, even if the student is much more proficient in his or her native language. For example, a student may feel much more comfortable speaking in Spanish but may have only been exposed to the math concept of "parallel lines" in English. If the student was presented a test item about parallel lines using a Spanish translation, he or she might not be able to demonstrate knowledge of that concept, given that the student was not familiar with the word for parallel lines in Spanish.

Side-by-Side English/Native-Language Test Versions

Having recognized these limitations of providing translated tests, many state assessment programs have developed (or are working to develop) test editions that involve side-by-side item presentation in the student's native language and English. This can ensure that students will have full access to the content of test items. Wolf et al. (2008) identified three studies that investigated the validity of a side-by-side translation accommodation; in two of the studies, it appeared that the dual-language version did not result in changes in test performance (Abedi, Courtney, Lean, Kao, & Azzam, 2006; Duncan et al., 2005). In the remaining study, the results suggested slight differences in test characteristics; however, they suggested that it may be due to differences in the groups who were tested under the given conditions rather than the testing change (Sireci & Khaliq, 2002). Although research has failed to suggest that this accommodation significantly increases the performance of groups of ELLs, it is important to recognize that it may provide better access for certain ELLs who are at a particular level of English language proficiency development. It is important to note that the challenges associated with translation still apply to this accommodation; back translation should be completed to ensure that the translation is appropriate. Without this effort, the student could be very confused by an item that seems to present something different in the two languages!

Bilingual Dictionaries/Glossaries/Word Lists

Offering bilingual dictionaries allows students to have access to translations of many words into their native language; bilingual glossaries or word lists provide translations as well, but only of those words that the student may encounter in the actual test items. In the research review by Francis et al. (2006), these accommodations appeared to have the least positive impact on student performance of those accommodations reviewed. However, it is important to recognize that it may still be a helpful accommodation for students who are at a particular stage in language development and have received instruction and practice on how to use these tools during instruction.

English Language Accommodations

In some cases, it is possible to effectively accommodate ELLs by providing them some additional support in English. Using this type of accommodation, substantial issues associated with translating the test or various words in the test can be avoided. However, it is important to be very careful about how English language accommodations are made so that they do not change the skills or concepts intended to be measured on the test.

Plain Language/Simplified English Language

An English language accommodation that is sometimes made available to ELLs is a plain language version of the test. Sometimes, test items have complicated or excessive wording and can be conveyed in a simplified format that may be much more accessible to students who are ELLs. Suggestions provided by the Council for Chief State School Officers (2002, pp. 43–44) for making items more accessible in plain language format to ELLs include the following:

- Use only brief, straightforward, simple sentences and stems.
- Use consistent paragraph structures throughout the assessment.
- Use present tense and active voice whenever possible.
- Paraphrasing of words or ideas should be kept to a minimum.
- Use pronouns judiciously.
- High-frequency words are the best choice.
- Words with double meanings and colloquialisms should be omitted or defined in text.

Just as in translating tests, it is important that a simplified English version of the test has the same meaning, and that no details that are important for responding correctly are omitted.

According to the Abedi et al. (2004) review, the language modification accommodation was one of the most beneficial of those investigated for ELLs. In the Francis et al. (2006) review, simplified English was found to be one of the most commonly studied ELL accommodations; however, it was not found to have a significant positive effect across all studies. Although there was no substantial evidence that it compromised the integrity of the test, there also was no strong evidence in support of it. It is important to recognize how the content of the test items may influence whether such an accommodation would be helpful; if the items include simple language to begin with, it may not be necessary to provide such an accommodated test version. In addition to the linguistic complexity of the items, individual differences in a student's level of English proficiency may determine whether this is an effective accommodation for any given student.

English Language Dictionary or Glossary

In contrast to providing a dictionary that provides a native language translation for words presented in English, students may be provided a dictionary or glossary of challenging words that would allow ELLs to better understand challenging English words that may be presented to them on the test. These may be either limited or extensive in content. A customized dictionary provides words on the test that are likely to be unfamiliar to many students. A summary of the research on test accommodations for ELLs identified customized English dictionaries to have a particularly positive impact on test performance among ELLs (Abedi et al., 2004).

A similar accommodation that would allow easier access to word meanings might involve providing definitions of words that students might not know in the margin of the test itself. Computerized tests can make it particularly easy for students to access related accommodations; hyperlinks can be added so that students can select and be immediately provided definitions for words that they do not know, which can reduce the amount of time that the student might have to otherwise spend looking up definitions. Abedi, Courtney, and Leon (2003) found that a computerized version of a math test that included such hyperlinks for difficult words was effective and valid for fourth- and eighth-grade ELLs. The Francis et al. (2006) review of accommodation effects found English language dictionaries and glossaries to have the most positive impact on test performance among ELLs.

Read-Aloud in English

Some ELLs may benefit from English language accommodations that are similar to those sometimes provided to students with disabilities, including having the test read aloud in English. Abedi at el. (2004) reviewed an unpublished study that suggested that some students may appreciate having the test read aloud to them in English if they have developed some conversational proficiency in English, but are not yet proficient at decoding and comprehending material written in English (Kopriva & Lowery, as cited in Abedi et al., 2004).

However, more investigation is needed to know the extent to which this accommodation may contribute to performance improvement among ELLs.

Nonlinguistic Accommodations

Additional accommodations that are not necessarily directly related to language presentation or response may be helpful for students who are ELLs.

Extended Time

Perhaps most commonly, extended time may be provided to allow ELLs the time necessary to process the English language. However, it is important to recognize that positive effects of this accommodation have been found for ELLs and non-ELLs alike (Abedi et al., 2004; Wolf et al., 2008), which may cause one to question whether it is fair to provide this accommodation only to ELLs. However, it is important to note that this accommodation may be needed to allow students to benefit from other accommodations, such as dictionaries, glossaries, and side-by-side translations of the test, which require extra time to use and to read. Many of the studies that have demonstrated positive effects of other accommodations for ELLs have included extended time in addition to the targeted accommodations.

Allowing More Test Breaks

Although research has not targeted the effects of this accommodation for ELLs, it is likely that the extra cognitive demands associated with understanding test items presented in a new language may make testing particularly fatiguing for ELLs. For some students, more frequent test breaks may be particularly helpful.

Setting Accommodations

Additional accommodations that often are provided to ELLs involve testing in a slightly different environment than the other students. These may include testing by their ESL or bilingual teacher and testing in small group format to avoid large group distractions. Although these have not been specifically targeted in the research literature, it may be the case that they are needed when applying other accommodations (i.e., read aloud, complete oral test translation, etc.).

IDENTIFYING THE LEAST RESTRICTIVE ACCOMMODATION PACKAGE

Each student may have a different set of accommodations that best promotes his or her access to the test and demonstration of skill and knowledge. A student's level of proficiency in English may be very important in determining what kinds of accommodations will be most effective. In addition, the student's level of competence and academic learning in his or her native language is also important in determining what may be the best accommodation package. Finally, the accommodations that the student receives and finds helpful during instruction are likely those that will also facilitate access to the test. In making accommodation decisions, it is very important for a variety of individuals to be involved in the process, including the student's teacher, parents, English language development (ELD) teacher, someone familiar with the statewide testing program, and the student himself or herself. In many cases, it will be important to take time to explain the purpose of statewide assessment, and the purpose of accommodations to parents of ELLs, given the language and cultural barriers that will likely be encountered. Having materials available in the family's native language or having a parent liaison who speaks the family's native language may be very helpful. The accommodations described in earlier sections of this chapter are just some of the accommodations that might be considered; there are certainly many other accommodations that may be helpful for a particular student and maintain the integrity of the test. However, it is important that the decisions be made based on the individual student's needs and characteristics. A study on the effects of a simplified English dictionary for LEP students suggested that the accommodation may be effective for some students but certainly not for all LEP students and recommended that such accommodation decisions be made on an individual basis (Albus, Bielinski, Thurlow, & Liu, 2001).

Although the decision-making team may come up with a set of accommodations that seems highly likely to be the best for the student at a particular point in time, it can be beneficial to "test out" whether those accommodations truly are helpful. Research has suggested individuals' perceptions of what may be effective accommodations for a particular student are not always accurate (Fuchs, Fuchs, Eaton, Hamlett, & Karns, 2000). Having the student try out a few combinations of accommodations that the team thinks may be particular helpful on a "mock" test may help identify what will be the most effective.

Recently, the selection taxonomy for English language learner accommodations (STELLA) was developed and tested (Kopriva, Emick, Hipolito-Delgado, & Cameron, 2007), with very positive results. STELLA is a computerized accommodation taxonomy for ELLs that takes into consideration a variety of student background characteristics and uses decision rules to determine which accommodation package would be most appropriate for the given student. When students were assigned accommodations based on STELLA, they tended to benefit more from the accommodations than when they were provided no accommodations and when they were provided accommodation packages not based on their individual needs, suggesting all the more for accommodations decisions to be made carefully, and with attention to the individual child's needs.

Once the team has identified which set of accommodations is optimal for the student, the team can examine whether the accommodations are considered "standard" for the statewide test. Many statewide assessment programs have policies about which accommodations are considered to maintain the integrity of the test for ELLs. The National Center on Educational Outcomes provides links to associated policies at *education.umn.edu/NCEO/LEP/Accommodations/StateLEPAccommPolicies.htm*. However, if the list of standard accommodations in your state does not include those that the team considers particularly helpful and appropriate for a given student, it is important to advocate for the given accommodation to be provided. Making contact with your state department about this can help ensure that policies are created that best help ELLs access testing.

ALIGNING INSTRUCTIONAL AND TESTING ACCOMMODATIONS

Although the focus of policies for statewide testing is on what accommodations can be provided on the test, it is important to recognize that in order for the student to make optimal use of an accommodation on the test, it should also be provided during instruction. This is important not only to ensure that the student is familiar with the accommodation, but also to be sure that the student has optimal access to teaching and learning in the content on which he or she is tested.

It is particularly important that students are familiar with dictionaries or glossaries that they may be provided during testing. If they are not familiar with these tools, they clearly will not be able to make optimal use of them, and provision of these tools on the test might then be considered worthless. With the development of recent technologies that can be provided on the computer, students of different native language backgrounds can more easily access information on what English words mean. It will be important for instruction and assessment to be aligned in terms of incorporating similar methods for students to access word meanings.

It is important to note, however, that in some circumstances it may be appropriate to make an accommodation available to a student during instruction, but not on the test. For example, an English/language arts test may be intended to test student vocabulary knowledge, and so providing help with word meanings would hinder measurement of the construct intended to be tested. However, during instruction, it would be very important for the teacher to provide word meanings so that the student could gain knowledge of what the word means. Altogether, it is important that the skills and knowledge targeted for testing are addressed during instruction, and that when possible and appropriate, similar formats and accommodations are made available across testing and instructional settings.

ENSURING APPROPRIATE LANGUAGE INSTRUCTION
WHILE PROVIDING ACCOMMODATIONS

One concern that many people have with providing language accommodations is that there will be less pressure for ELLs to learn English as a result of being provided related assistance. If students always have access to a translated version of the test, there may be less pressure placed on schools to have them gain English language proficiency. Currently, competence in English is needed across many settings for students to be successful in the United States. It is considered very important for students to learn to read and speak English in elementary and secondary schools. It is therefore important to ensure that students have access to quality instruction to learn the English language while they are being provided accommodations for testing.

In many circumstances, the provision of an accommodation can actually facilitate English language learning. For instance, providing accommodations such as side-by-side translations, glossaries, and dictionaries may actually help students learn English. The more accessible such tools are, the more likely students will use them and learn English. Related computerized accommodations are particularly helpful, given that students can often learn word meanings through a mere click of the computer mouse.

EVALUATING WHETHER A CHANGE IN ACCOMMODATIONS IS NEEDED

Given that one goal is for ELLs to eventually become literate and fluent in English, it is expected that their language proficiency will develop over time, and they will eventually no longer need support for understanding material presented in English. As students progress in the development of English language proficiency, they will require fewer supports to understand test content. In fact, if certain accommodations continue to be provided when they are no longer necessary, they may actually hinder students from performing optimally. For instance, students may initially benefit from a native language translation if they have had substantial prior academic instruction in their native language and have just recently moved to the United States. However, as they begin to develop English language skills, and learn new concepts in the English language, it may be more appropriate for them to take the test in English with various supports (e.g., side-by-side translation, English glossary, etc.). As they become proficient in English, they may move into needing extended time to process the language, and eventually progress to being able to best complete the test under standard conditions. Depending on a variety of student characteristics and quality of instruction, it may take some students much longer to go through this progression of decreasing support. It is therefore important to consider each student's needs individually, and on a regular basis. At a minimum, this should occur each year before the test is administered, but optimally would occur more frequently in order to make sure that the student is provided the appropriate level of support during instruction, as well. Cummins's (1984) work suggests that it typically will take 5 years or more for a student to develop CALP, and so it can be expected that the student may need some level of support and accommodation for understanding English in the academic realm for that period of time (or potentially more!).

STUDENTS WITH DISABILITIES WHO ARE ELLS

It is important to recognize that many students who are ELLs may also be students with disabilities and therefore have multiple accommodation needs. The proportion of ELLs who have disabilities is likely to be similar to the proportion of all students who have disabilities (i.e., approximately 12% of all students). Identifying ELLs who have disabilities can be a very complicated process. In some cases, students who simply have not mastered English proficiency may be erroneously identified as having a disability. In other cases, ELLs who truly have disabilities may be not identified, given that school professionals simply consider their difficulties to be language-related. It is important for school professionals to use great care when evaluating ELLs for special education eligibility. Based on evaluation results, there may be very different guidelines for the types of accommodations that the student may receive and have considered to maintain the integrity of a test.

When making accommodation decisions for ELLs with disabilities, it is important for all individuals who provide services to the student to be involved in decision making (i.e., ELD teacher, special education teacher, parents, student, general education teacher, someone familiar with statewide test, etc.). It can also be important and helpful to have someone who knows the student's native language available to help explain what the test is about and the importance of making good accommodation decisions. Language-related and other accommodations may be needed for the student to have access to demonstrating knowledge and skill in an appropriate manner. These can best be determined by taking into consideration the guidelines provided in the previous sections on accommodating students with disabilities and accommodating ELLs. One important difference in testing for ELLs with disabilities in comparison to other students with disabilities is that they may need to participate in a mandated English language proficiency test. Accommodations for this test may need to be determined separate from those for the other statewide tests, given that language proficiency is the subject area targeted, and therefore English language accommodations may not be appropriate.

One challenge that has been identified in accommodating ELLs with disabilities by those who develop policies at the state level for such populations is finding individuals who can provide live translations or interpretations of statewide tests for students in their native language who also have a strong understanding of the needs of students with disabilities (Anderson, Minnema, Thurlow, & Hall-Lande, 2005). Furthermore, such individuals may need training to ensure that they understand the importance of presenting the test content in a standardized, unbiased manner so that appropriate results can be obtained. Just as it has been suggested that there be clear guidelines provided for readers, scribes, and sign-language interpreters (Clapper et al., 2005), it will be helpful to provide guidelines for accommodation provision to those who may help to provide language and disability-related accommodations to ELLs.

CASE EXAMPLE: ASAD

In Chapter 2, we provided an example of how a participation decision was made for a student who was an ELL (see pp. 31–32). In this section we illustrate a similar process, but provide an example of an ELL who requires more extensive accommodations.

Asad is a 16-year-old ninth grader who is originally from Somalia. He came to the United States when he was 14 years old. Prior to moving to the United States, Asad's education had been sporadic. He had received some education between the ages of 7 and 12 but then did not receive any consistent education between the time he was 12 and 14 years of age. Somali is his native language. However, he was instructed primarily in Arabic, although he did receive some instruction in English when living in Somalia. For the past 2 years, he has received all academic instruction in English; however, his ESL teacher has been providing extensive support to him and his teachers in all content areas to help him understand the concepts. Although he is making progress in learning English, and ultimately wants to learn English and be accepted into a top-notch college in the United States, he currently remains substantially below proficiency in English. His ESL teacher typically finds ways to present material from his content area coursework in both Arabic and English, as much as she is able. Follow along with the decision-making framework in Figure 4.1 to determine how Asad was to participate in the statewide assessment program. A blank version of the form can be found in Appendix 2.2.

Participation Decision-Making Form
for English Language Learners

Is this student also a student with a disability? <u>No.</u> If yes, complete the Participation Decision-Making Form for Students with Disabilities (Appendix 2.1), and then return to complete this form, along with the Accommodation Decision-Making Form for Students with Disabilities (Appendix 3.3).

It may be helpful to attach the following to this form, and provide copies to team members:
- a copy of the grade-level content, achievement, modified, and alternate achievement standards
- information on the testing format for the regular assessment and alternate assessment
- list of accommodations considered standard in your state
- information on any consequences associated with test participation (e.g., student not eligible for merit awards, standard diploma, etc.)

Student name: <u>Asad Ahmed</u>　　　　Date of birth: <u>1992</u>　　　　Grade: <u>9</u>

School: <u>Washington High</u>　　　　Date form completed: <u>January 9, 2008</u>

No. of years that the student will have been enrolled in a U.S. school by testing day: <u>2</u>

Team members participating (their role): <u>Asad Ahmed (student), Ayan and Dalmar Ahmed (parents),</u>
<u>Julie Jefferson (Asad's general education teacher), Ghedi Jumali (English as a second language specialist),</u>
<u>Jonah White (counselor)</u>

Checklist

X All team members have an understanding of the purpose of the accountability assessment

X All team members have examined the content standards and grade-level achievement standards

X All team members are familiar with the format of the regular assessment

X All team members are aware of consequences associated with having the student participate under nonstandard conditions

X All team members know that the student will participate in an English Language Proficiency Test

How is the student currently instructed? (mark an "X")

Content area	English	Other language	Combination
Math			X
English/language arts			X
Social studies			X
Science			X

How has the student been instructed in the past, and for how long? *(mark years in boxes)*

Content area	English	Other language	Combination
Math		5 years	2 years
English/language arts		5 years	2 years
Social studies		5 years	2 years
Science		5 years	2 years

(continued)

FIGURE 4.1. Completed example for Asad of the Participation Decision-Making Form for English Language Learners.

Considering what you have provided in the tables above, which should be the focus of presentation of the regular assessment for this student?

Content area	English	Other language	Combination
Math			X
English/language arts	X		
Social studies			X
Science			X

Note. *English/language arts must be administered in English if the student has been enrolled in a public school for more than one year.*

If other language was marked, what specific other language accommodations will be used? (see Appendix 2.2)

Asad will receive English and Arabic versions of the math, social studies, and science tests. Because he is not yet proficient in English, and he regularly receives Arabic translations of class materials to make progress in his content area coursework, this seems appropriate at this time.

What additional accommodations will be needed for the student to perform well according to the selected language of presentation? (see Appendix 2.2)

Extra time is considered necessary, given that he may need extra time to go back and forth between the test forms in order to read the items such that he understands what each is asking.

Has the student used these accommodations before?   (Yes)   No*

If "no" was indicated above, what is the plan for familiarizing the student with these accommodations?

Is training needed for individuals to help with providing accommodations (e.g., a reader, a scribe, an interpreter)?   __ yes   X_ no

If yes, who will oversee this training? _____

Who will be responsible for ensuring that these accommodations are available to the student on the day of testing? Ghedi Jumali (English as a second language specialist)

Note. If the ELL is also a student with a disability, also fill out Accommodation Decision-Making Form (Appendix 2.2). Not applicable.

FIGURE 4.1. (*continued*)

5

Alternate Assessments
for Students with Disabilities

A small, but meaningful, percentage of students with disabilities are unable to participate in general state and districtwide tests even with testing accommodations. Because of the educational challenges and difficulties caused by their disabilities, the resulting large-scale assessment scores for this group of students would be inaccurate portrayals of their academic achievement. In cases where testing accommodations are inadequate to facilitate inclusion, alternate assessments are developed and implemented to facilitate the participation of students with significant disabilities in accountability systems. In fact, alternate assessments have been described as the "ultimate accommodation" for promoting the inclusion of students in standards-based assessment and school reform efforts (Roach, 2005).

This chapter provides an overview of a number of key concepts in understanding and implementing alternate assessments based on alternate achievement standards (AA-AAS). In addition, the chapter briefly introduces two other forms of alternate assessments (i.e., alternate assessments based on modified achievement standards and alternate assessments based on general achievement standards) that are currently less prevalent in state accountability systems.

ALTERNATE ASSESSMENTS BASED ON ALTERNATE
ACHIEVEMENT STANDARDS

Because alternate assessments are an important component of each state's assessment and accountability system, they are required to meet the federal regulations outlined in Title I of the Elementary and Secondary Education Act. Specifically, Title I mandates that "State assessment shall be aligned with the State's challenging content and student performance standards and provide coherent information about student attainment of such standards" (§1111[b][3][B]). Moreover, NCLB requires a disaggregated annual reporting of students' performance to insure that all groups (including students with significant disabilities) are making adequate progress toward the goal of *all* students being "proficient" on statewide assessments by 2014 (Elliott & Roach, 2007).

Subsequent interpretations of the NCLB requirements by the U.S. Department of Education (2003) have attempted to create flexibility in this requirement by allowing up to 1% of students in states, school districts, and schools to demonstrate "proficient" performance via participation in statewide AA-AAS. Taking advantage of this flexibility, however, requires that a state's AA-AAS be a technically adequate measure of students' achievement of the same rigorous academic content expected of *all* students. Many states initially struggled to develop AA-AAS that met these requirements because (1) the skills and concepts in the state academic standards were considered inappropriate or irrelevant for students with significant disabilities; (2) assessment strategies for evaluating these students' academic skills were not familiar to many educators, test developers, and policymakers; and (3) the development of the alternate assessment was considered a special education function and therefore only nominally connected to the state's overall assessment and accountability system (Roach & Elliott, 2006).

Prior to the mandate to develop alternate assessments, the majority of system-level information collected and reported regarding students with significant disabilities focused on prevalence of disabilities, compliance with evaluation and placement procedures, and categorical descriptors of the educational programming offered by schools and districts (Turner, Baldwin, Kleinert, & Kearns, 2000). Because of this, policymakers and the public generally had limited information on schools' progress in providing meaningful and effective curriculum and instruction for students with significant disabilities (Ysseldyke, Thurlow, McGrew, & Vanderwood, 1994). The systematic consideration of alternate assessment results and their relationship to other measures of program quality and educational outcomes provides an opportunity to improve our understanding of efforts to extend standards-based reform and research-validated instruction to students with significant disabilities.

Determining Which Students Participate in AA-AAS

An essential element in creating an alternate assessment system is the development of a meaningful decision-making framework for determining which students qualify for participation in an AA-AAS. Specifically, IDEA instructs states to develop "guidelines for the participation of students in alternate assessment for those children who cannot participate in state and district-wide assessment programs" (§300.138; Part B). In addition, IDEA requires documenting in students' IEPs the justification for exclusion from the general large-scale assessment and a description of how the students will be assessed using an alternate method.

In response to this requirement, states have developed a wide variety of frameworks for identifying students with disabilities who should participate in alternate assessments. Typically, states have chosen to use a checklist (or series of questions) that is completed by participants in students' IEP meetings. These decision-making templates vary widely across states, ranging from a few general questions regarding a student's level of functioning to extensive, multistep procedures that require consideration of the students' curriculum and documentation of needed testing and instructional accommodations (see Table 5.1).

TABLE 5.1. AA-AAS Participation Criteria across Six States

Participation criterion	DE	VA	SC	LA	KY	WI
Student cannot complete academic curricula even with modifications and accommodations.	X	X			X	X
Student requires extensive direct instruction in multiple settings to accomplish application and transfer of skills.	X	X	X		X	X
Student is unable to use academic skills at a minimal competency level with instructed through typical classroom instruction.	X					
Student's difficulties with the regular academic curricula are not the result of extensive absences or social, cultural, or economic differences.	X		X	X	X	X
Student is unable to acquire, maintain, or generalize skills and demonstrate performance without intense, individualized instruction.	X, above 14 years old only	X	X	X	X	
Student works to an expectation that differs in complexity from grade-level expectations.			X			X
Student has current IEP.		X			X	
Student is working toward educational goals other than those prescribed for a modified standard, standard, or advanced studies diploma program.		X, high school only			X	
Student's impairments cause dependence on others for most, if not all, daily living needs, and the student is expected to require extensive ongoing support in adulthood.				X		
Student's instructional program emphasizes life skills and functional applications of the general education curriculum.				X		
Current longitudinal data (e.g., classroom observation, task analyses, progress of IEP objectives, evaluations, and parental information) indicate the student should participate in alternate assessment.				X		

In some states, IEP teams may determine that students with disabilities do not qualify for an alternate assessment in all subject domains. In these cases, team members must decide whether it is reasonable to use the alternate assessment for some subjects and administer an alternate assessments based on modified achievement standards (AA-MAS; discussed later in this chapter) or an accommodated large-scale standardized assessment in others.

Under NCLB, states and school districts may include no more than 1% of students' performance on AA-AAS as "proficient" for AYP calculations, thus it is essential that IEP teams identify the *right* students for participation in AA-AAS. To make informed decisions about the appropriateness of AA-AAS for an individual student, IEP teams need to be familiar with the format and content of their state's general large-scale assessment as well as their state's policies on testing accommodations and AA-MAS. In many states, data from the initial implementation of AA-AAS suggest IEP teams are identifying significantly less than 1% of students to participate in alternate assessment across subjects and grade levels.

Insuring Reliable and Valid Decisions Based on AA-AAS Results

Some states' AA-AAS have limited evidence for the reliability and validity of their resulting scores. Without documentation of the technical adequacy of an alternate assessment, serious questions may be raised about using the resulting scores for (1) monitoring educational performance at the levels of student, classroom, school, and system and (2) making decisions about the effectiveness of curriculum and instruction. Moreover, in the case of students with significant disabilities, some educators may worry that narrowing of the enacted curriculum and deemphasis of other important educational outcomes (e.g., self-determination or social skills) will be unintended consequences of their inclusion in schools' and states' AYP reporting (Baker & Linn, 2002).

In some states, the original approach to AA-AAS involved a review of student performance similar to what typically might be part of a reevaluation procedure or an IEP process. This approach, however, resulted in students with significant cognitive disabilities receiving idiographic (i.e., individualized) assessments that were neither standards focused nor easily aggregated for AYP reporting. In discussing IEP reviews, Thurlow and colleagues (1996) stated, "The primary problem with this approach is that attainment of IEP goals cannot be easily aggregated for accountability purposes and IEP goals do not serve as a total curriculum for a student" (p. 18).

Because functional and adaptive behaviors are often the focus of IEP goals for students with significant disabilities, many students' AA-AAS would not have reflected the range of knowledge and skills identified by states' academic standards (Roach, 2005). In light of the difficulties with this approach to alternate assessment, the most recent review of state's assessment programs indicated only 4% were currently using IEP reviews for alternate assessment (Thompson, Johnstone, et al., 2005).

Conversely, the most recent National Center of Education Outcomes review of states' alternate assessment practices indicates 50% of states were implementing some form of portfolio assessments (Thompson, Johnstone, et al., 2005). The most recent review of state alternate assessment practices also indicates that 14% of states are using a rating scale or checklist as part of their AA-AAS. In most cases, these rating scales require the collection of an accompanying body of classroom-based evidence to support the scoring procedure. In fact, there is considerable "overlap" between the various AA-AAS approaches. As Thompson, Johnstone, and colleagues stated in their review:

> It may be that the traditional way of describing alternate assessment approaches is no longer the best because there is considerable overlap across approaches that states take. For example, of the 25 states using portfolio (body of evidence) assessments in 2005, 13 states use a standardized set of performance events, tasks, or skills. Three of the seven states using a rating scale of performance on a standardized set of events, tasks, or skills require the submission of a body of evidence. (p. 11)

Rating scales, performance assessments, and portfolios are appealing because of their potential to provide rich, multifaceted descriptions of students' real-life knowledge and skills (Elliott & Fuchs, 1997). Each of these approaches, however, is dependent (at least to some degree) on teacher observations and decision making. These approaches often ask teachers to determine which skills and concepts to cover in an assessment, which evidence to collect and include, and how best to characterize students' independence and accuracy in completing tasks.

The participation and responsibilities expected of teachers (and other educators) in completing AA-AAS are very different from their involvement in large-scale assessments given to the majority of students. Fortunately, a substantial body of evidence on the validity of teachers' judgments of student behavior and academic performance provides support for these approaches. A review of the literature on teacher judgments of students' academic performance by Hoge and Coladarci (1989) found direct teacher judgments (i.e., ratings that entailed the use of explicit performance criterion) yielded a median correlation of .70. In the same review, studies that included indirect teacher judgments (i.e., ratings of student achievement without explicit definitions or behavior or skills to be evaluated) produced a median correlation of .62. In both cases, the correlations exceeded the convergent and concurrent validity coefficients reported for many widely used educational tests.

Another concern regarding AA-AAS is that problems establishing the reliability of ratings may negatively influence students' and schools' outcome scores. For example, initial data from Kentucky's alternate assessment development efforts suggested reliability of scores may represent a significant challenge for states using portfolios—or other methods that include ratings of student work—for their AA-AAS (Browder, Fallin, Davis, & Karvonen, 2003). This result is similar to the difficulties in establishing reliable ratings previously observed in states attempting to use portfolios and performance assessments as part of their general large-scale assessment systems (Koertz, McCaffrey, Klein, & Bell, 1993; Tindal et al., 2003). When interrater reliability or agreement cannot be established, states may not be able to publicly report AA-AAS results or include the result in AYP reporting.

Tindal et al. (2003) have conducted research on extended reading and math tasks, which provide an intriguing option for conducting an alternate assessment. This approach consists of continua of tasks that measure students' basic skills in reading and mathematics. Assessors guide students through increasingly difficult assessment tasks, stopping when it is clear that no additional accurate and meaningful information on their performance will be obtained. Tindal and colleagues examined the performance of 437 students who were administered extended reading and mathematics tasks by trained administrators, providing evidence for the reliability of this approach. Trained raters were asked to examine the assessment protocols and provide qualitative ratings of the students' overall performance in reading and mathematics. The reliability (i.e., interrater agreement) of these ratings was excellent: nearly 100% of the ratings were in exact agreement or within 1 point (on a 6-point rubric) in both subject areas. A key take-away message from this research is the necessity of effective training for individuals who are expected to administer and/or score AA-AAS. This sort of preparation increases the likelihood that AA-AAS are given correctly and scored accurately.

Moreover, to demonstrate adequate alignment to state standards, portfolios and performance assessments may need to include numerous tasks and work samples. The mandate to create a portfolio or performance assessment system that aligns to the scope of grade-level standards may result in an extensive and time-consuming assessment process. Because they often include items that tap a broader range of skills, ratings that are scale-based in various states have been judged as adequately aligned to state content standards using a modification of the nationally recognized Webb approach to alignment analysis (see Roach et al., 2005, for an example). AA-AAS based on rating scales often are supported by classroom-based evidence samples, however, which might result in the same alignment difficulties experienced by portfolio- and performance-based AA-AAS. To address some of the alignment challenges for AA-AAS, Flowers, Wakeman, Browder, and Karvonen (2007) have developed a more extensive revision of the Webb's alignment process called Links of Academic Learning (LAL). "The LAL model goes beyond examining the degree of match between standards and (AA-AAS) to consider other criteria relevant for students with significant cognitive disabilities" (p. 9). The LAL criteria include consideration of whether:

1. The content measured on AA-AAS in academic in nature and included core content areas (e.g., reading/language arts, mathematic, science).
2. The content reflects students' grade-level curriculum.
3. The focus of achievement maintains "fidelity" to the actual grade-level standards.
4. The content differs from grade-level standards in terms of range and complexity of concepts and skills.
5. The AA-AAS includes differentiation across grade levels or grade bands (i.e., the same tasks and skills are not required at each grade level).
6. Potential barriers or sources of challenge to student performance are minimized.
7. The expected level of achievement on the AA-AAS is for students to demonstrate learning of grade-reference materials.
8. The instructional program and materials promote access to the general curriculum.

Although this alignment method is relatively new, the LAL holds promise for providing more comprehensive and applicable evaluations of alignment for the various forms of AA-AAS being implemented across the United States.

Browder, Fallin, et al.'s (2003) review of the AA-AAS literature also includes student risk factors (e.g., instability of student behavior or health status) as potential threats to the validity and reliability of decisions based on students' alternate assessment results. For example, when assessments include on-demand performance of various skills, fluctuations in student behavior or physical well-being might negatively affect students' scores, resulting in inaccurate and invalid inferences about their achievement and understanding. To address this difficulty, AA-AAS scores should be based on multiple observations and/or opportunities for students to demonstrate their skills and knowledge.

AA-AAS: Functional-Focused versus Standards-Based

IDEA clearly mandates that students with disabilities should have access to the general education curriculum and academic standards. Specifically, students' IEPs must include consideration of how the student will access the general education curriculum (§300.347). Moreover, this section of IDEA requires that all students have opportunities and instruction that allow them to make progress toward learning the skills and concepts outlined in state and district academic content standards. Additional information on facilitating curricular access in provided in a later chapter in this text.

This emphasis on instruction and curriculum based on grade-level academic standards represents a dramatic departure from the educational practices traditional implemented with many students with significant disabilities. After the passage of Public Law 94-142, special education programs initially focused on providing developmental curricula for students with significant disabilities. Early special education curricula often comprised materials and tasks based on students' "assessment-derived" mental ages (e.g., stringing beads, stacking blocks) without consideration of the age or grade appropriateness. In response to the limitations of this approach, special educators abandoned developmental curricula and moved toward the "criterion of ultimate functioning," designing and implementing functional curricula to addressed students' self-care, social, and vocational needs (Browder, Spooner, et al., 2003).

Over the past 20 years, many educators and parents have worked toward increased integration and inclusion of students with significant disabilities in general education settings. These efforts often have targeted the social skill and self-esteem benefits for students, but more recent practices have added an emphasis on exposure to and experiences with the general curriculum and the broader school experience (Ford, Davern, & Schnorr, 2001). Educators should understand, however, that the most recent federal legislation (i.e., NCLB and IDEA) demand an even greater access to general education contexts and curricula. These laws continue to endorse the right of each student with disabilities to individualized programming, but they also demand more than merely being present in a general education classroom for compliance. Progress toward and achievement of skills and knowledge outlined in grade-level general education standards is now a mandated outcome (Pugach & Warger, 2001). Therefore, students with significant disabilities must have instruction and accommodations that promote their progress (no matter how modest) toward the educational expectations of the larger student population (Roach & Elliott, 2006).

A related concern is the content and focus of each state's AA-AAS processes. Specifically, educators and family members must understand that AA-AAS systems must be focused on the content standards identified for *all* students. Some educators will argue that if AA-AAS are intended to measure the most salient elements of curriculum and instruction for students with significant disabilities, these tests should focus on functional and adaptive behaviors. Although there may be some merit to this argument, if the AA-AAS are intended to be part of the larger accountability system and facilitate progress in the core curriculum areas (i.e., reading, mathematics, science), then a state's academic standards must form the foundation for the alternate assessment. This sentiment seems to be reflected in states' efforts to develop and refine their alternate assessment practices. "In 1999, 32% of states were using only functional skills for their AA-AAS with no link to state standards, by 2001 only 8% were doing so" (Browder, Fallin, Davis, & Karvonen, 2003, p. 259). A 2005 National Center on Education Outcomes survey of state departments of education indicated 60% of states were using grade-level content standards as the basis for their AA-AAS or creating extended content standards that were "linked" to grade-level content (Thompson, Johnstone, et al., 2005).

Researchers and policymakers have begun to give more attention to the legislative mandate to align AA-AAS with states' grade-level content standards. Browder et al. (2004) examined the performance indicators from 31 states' alternate assessment systems, reviewing three separate curricular domains: language arts, mathematics, and functional. Review panels included teachers, parents, and nationally recognized experts in various curriculum domains and special education. Each reviewer received an open-ended survey of 12 items asking him or her to provide feedback on the developmental level, curricular focus, and functional utility of the performance indicators listed. Reviewers then participated in a focus group (composed of either experts or stakeholders) where they reviewed their survey responses and developed summaries of the key themes in their reviews. Nearly all the experts and stakeholders reported that some states' performance indicators were clearly aligned to language arts and mathematics standards. There was an equal level of agreement among both groups that other states' performance indicators did not reflect the content of the standards.

Browder, Spooner, et al. (2003) extended the Browder et al. (2004) study by completing a quantitative analysis of six states' performance indicators in language arts and mathematics. Performance indicators included those identified by the previous study as having varying levels of alignment: clear alignment, weak, or mixed. Two members of the research team coded the curricular philosophy reflected by the task and context (e.g., material, environment) for a list of 987 performance indicators. Categories of curricular philosophy (i.e., coding options) included developmental/early childhood, functional, social inclusion/social communication, self-determination, and academic. Interrater agreement for the coding of curricular philosophy was 93% for tasks and 94% for contexts. The results indicated states whose performance indicators were identified in the Browder et al. (2004) study as clearly aligned included more indicators that were coded as academic, whereas weakly aligned states included more performance indicators in the functional and other categories.

This should not be taken, however, as an indication that functional skills are no longer important for students who take an AA-AAS. Ford et al. (2001) stated, "acknowledging that a central purpose of [AA-AAS] is to measure major, agreed-upon outcomes over time does not take away from extensive and ongoing learning that is not captured in these assessments" (p. 214). Indeed, much as we do not expect multiple-choice standardized tests to measure the entire scope of curriculum and instruction provided to general education students, we should not expect AA-AAS to reflect every important element of the school experiences of students with significant disabilities (Roach et al., 2005).

The Bottom Line: AA-AAS Technical Adequacy Is Essential!

Regardless of the type of assessment strategy selected for use by state policymakers, development of alternate assessment instruments must include investigations to establish the instruments' technical adequacy. Alternate assessment scores are useful or good to the extent that the assessment: (1) measures what the students have been studying in their classes, (2) is aligned to state content standards, and (3) results in scores that are consistent and accurate. To the extent that the AA-AAS measures subject matter content that is different from what students have been studying, students' test scores become less meaningful as measures of their academic progress and less useful in guiding teachers' future instructional efforts. Likewise, if the students' performance and progress cannot be determined consistently and accurately, teachers' and other stakeholders' confidence in the results of AA-AAS will be lessened.

CASE EXAMPLE OF AN AA-AAS: GERALDO

In this case example, we will illustrate the Mississippi Alternate Assessment of Extended Curriculum Frameworks (MAAECF) for students with significant cognitive disabilities. The MAAECF is designed to assess the educational performance of students with disabilities who cannot meaningfully take all or part of the Mississippi Content Tests (MCT) even with accommodations. Most students who participate in the MAAECF typically are working on curriculum that typically knowledge and skills that are extensions of or prerequisites to the grade-level general education curriculum.

Student Information

Geraldo is in the seventh grade and is 14 years old. He has been identified was having autism and a cognitive disability and is served in a self-contained classroom at his middle school. He also has a hearing impairment and receives speech–language services. He has difficulty maintaining eye contact and consistently interacting with others.

Current Instructional Plan

Geraldo enjoys school and has a pleasant disposition. He is agile and demonstrates no difficulties with either fine or gross motor skills. He can dress and feed himself and uses the bathroom independently (including toileting and washing hands). Geraldo often communicates his needs by pointing to what he wants (e.g., food items). He interacts with a few toys (balls and a popcorn toy) and basic educational computer programs. Geraldo can match, sort, and categorize (two to three fields) with objects and pictures.

Geraldo receives a number instructional supports and accommodations. He uses augmentative communication devices in all subject areas in the self-contained classroom and mainstreamed settings. Geraldo participates in general education classrooms during art, physical education, and music. In these contexts, he also is provided with an instructional assistant to facilitate his participation.

Criteria for Participation in the AA-AAS

To participate in the MAAECF for students with disabilities, Geraldo's IEP team had to complete the MAAECF Participation Checklist (see Figure 5.1) to determine if he met four criteria individually for language arts and mathematics. In the case of Geraldo's IEP team, it was noted that the IEP included information on his present level of performance in reference to the Mississippi state content standards. In addition, the IEP team had a good working knowledge of the test format and what skills and knowledge are being measured by the MCT statewide assessment. Geraldo's IEP team also was knowledgeable regarding the state testing guidelines and the use of appropriate testing accommodations when necessary. In Geraldo's case, the IEP team made a decision that he was unable to participate in the MCT even with accommodations. Once his team made this decision, the MAAECF process began.

The MAAECF Process

Geraldo's IEP team participated in the completion of the MAAECF. The MAAECF process was completed by his special education teacher with data collection assistance from the instructional aide, speech therapist, and Geraldo's mother. Geraldo's special education teacher completed the MAAECF ratings because she had firsthand knowledge of his IEP goals, objectives, and benchmarks, educational curriculum, and current level of educational functioning.

• *Step 1*: In Geraldo's case, his teacher completed the MAAECF for language arts and mathematics subject areas. The first step in completing the MAAECF process involved collecting at least two types of evidence to use when rating items within each item cluster. The classroom- and community-based evidence was collected to provide a "picture of performance" on a skill or set of skills being assessed by each MAAECF item cluster. On the MAAECF for grades 6–8, there are 12 to 13 item clusters in each content area; therefore, for middle school students, 12 to 13 sets of evidence must be submitted for each content area. Other educators (e.g., the instructional aide, speech therapist) and Geraldo's family assisted in collecting some of these evidence samples. Geraldo's teacher used the MAAECF Evidence Worksheets (see Appendix 5-1) to organize collection and documentation of the evidence. There are four types of worksheets for (1) Observation Evidence, (2) Work Samples

Mississippi Alternative Assessment
of Extended Curriculum Frameworks Participation Checklist

Student: _Geraldo_ _____   MSIS#: _____   Date: _3-18-200X_ _____

IEP team members are responsible for deciding which students with disabilities participate in the regular assessment, with or without testing accommodations, or in the state's alternate assessment for students with significant cognitive disabilities. To complete this decision-making process, IEP team members must:

- Have current knowledge of the student's general performance level relative to the state's academic content standards.
- Be knowledgeable of the statewide achievement test format and the skills and knowledge it measures.
- Be knowledgeable of state testing guidelines and the use of appropriate testing accommodations.

To facilitate informed and equitable decision making, IEP teams should address each of the following statements *for each of the academic content areas* when considering an alternate assessment. If the IEP team concurs that all four of the statements below accurately characterize a student's current educational situation, then an alternate assessment should be used to provide a meaningful evaluation of the student's current academic achievement. Check all statements that apply to the student named above.

Participation Criteria	Language Arts	Math	Science
1. The student's curriculum and daily instruction focus on knowledge and skills significantly below his/her chronological grade level and focus on content typical of that in the state's expanded content standards document.	X	X	X
2. The student's present level of educational performance significantly impedes participation in and completion of the grade-level general education curriculum even with significant modifications to the instructional program and materials.	X	X	X
3. The student requires extensive, individualized direct instruction to accomplish the acquisition, application, and transfer of knowledge and skills.	X	X	X
4. The student's difficulty with the regular curriculum demands is primarily due to his/her disabilities, and not to excessive absences unrelated to the disability, or social, cultural, or environmental factors.	X	X	X

Participation Decision Summary: _____

_____

_____

FIGURE 5.1. Completed example for Geraldo of the MAAECF Participation Checklist. From Mississippi Department of Education (2008); *http://www.mde.k12.ms.us/maaecf/*.

or Test Results Evidence, (3) Interview-Based Evidence, and (4) Media Recorded Evidence. At least two of these worksheets (with accompanying evidence samples) must be used in assessing each item cluster.

- *Step 2*: Geraldo's teacher completed ratings for every item on MAAECF rating scale, using the MAAECF item proficiency rating rubric to rate the student's level of proficiency for all of the items in each content areas assessed. Brief descriptions of the four levels of item proficiency are as follows:

0 = Nonexistent (can't do currently)
1 = Emerging (aware and starting to do)
2 = Progressing (can do partially and inconsistently)
3 = Accomplished (can do well and consistently)

Additional descriptive criteria for making item-level decision are providing in the MAAECF rubric.

• *Step 3*: Geraldo's teacher placed all the evidence samples and the accompanying MAAECF Evidence Worksheets in an accordion folder for final submission (see Appendix 5.1). The MAAECF rating scale and the folder with Geraldo's evidence sample were given to the school district's special education coordinator for submission to the state's centralized scoring center.

• *Step 4*: At the state's centralized scoring center, Geraldo's evidence was reviewed and rated by an independent rater who was an experienced special educator or administrator. First, the scoring center staff calculated mean item cluster scores based on Geraldo's teacher's ratings (which ranged from 0 to 3). For example, an item cluster with five items with ratings of 2, 2, 3, 1, and 1 would have a mean Item Cluster Rating of 1.8; for purposes of determining agreement with an independent rater, this mean would be rounded to 2. An independent rater at the scoring center then rated each item cluster 0, 1, 2, or 3 based on the evidence samples submitted by Geraldo's teacher. Agreement between the teacher's and independent rater's cluster scores was determined for one randomly selected content scale. If there was acceptable agreement, then the teacher's cluster scores were used for accountability purposes. If not the level of agreement was not acceptable, then all content scales were scored by the first independent rater and a second rater at the Scoring Center. Their mean cluster scores would then replace those of Geraldo's teacher. After scoring at the scoring center, Geraldo's teacher received feedback about the quality of the evidence she collected and the reliability of the ratings.

• *Step 5*: Using cut scores set by the MAAECF standard setting process (*note: A "new" standards setting institute will occur in Summer 2008 to reset cut scores for each of the MAAECF performance levels*), the results of Geraldo's ratings for each content area were translated to an Overall Performance Level by placing the correct Total Individualized Proficiency Score on the score continuum below the Performance Level descriptions (see Figure 5.2 for an example). The Performance Level descriptions from the content area provide a four-level, criterion-referenced continuum that characterizes performance of knowledge and skills along the path toward functioning at or near grade level in the regular curriculum. Thus, based on the Individualized Proficiency Score for each content area assessed, Geraldo's performance could be summarized as "not yet proficient" in language arts and mathematics for AYP performing.

Summary

In Geraldo's case, the MAAECF provided an opportunity to participate in an alternate assessment that measured his progress toward meeting educational goals on state standards

Grades 6–8 Language Arts

Language arts involves development of skills and understanding of concepts in five interrelated strands: (1) reading, (2) writing, (3) speaking, (4) listening, and (5) viewing. The skills and concepts in these five strands vary in complexity and importance for students at each grade level. A critical component at each grade level is text complexity in terms of sophistication of language, content, and syntax. As students progress through the grades, the skills and concepts required to comprehend and compose texts become increasingly complex.

To develop and demonstrate skills in language arts, students require varying levels of support especially as text complexity increases. This support or accommodation is intended to facilitate access and/or responds of knowledge and skills the student has developed.

Minimal	Basic	Proficient	Advanced
Student is able to perform simple skills but has difficulty in communicating understanding and demonstrating most discrete preliteracy skills. Student currently exhibits one or two of the entry-level skills and knowledge in reading at a barely *emerging* level. Student typically: • Demonstrates very limited understanding of the most basic language arts concepts and skills. • Attends and responds to texts that are read to him or her by an adult or peer. • Communicates personal wants, needs, and opinions verbally or through the use of assistive technology.	Student attends to language arts instruction and participates in activities. Student responds or performs several skills in at least one language arts strand, typically at the *emerging* level in at least one setting. Student typically can: • Notice pictures in text and use them to make inferences and predictions. • Attend to and demonstrate an understanding of texts that are read to him or her by an adult or peer. • Use a basic sight vocabulary and phonological skills to read unfamiliar words or texts.	Student demonstrates the ability to communicate ideas and decode and comprehend text. The student's understanding of basic concepts and performance of many skills in two or three language arts strands are typically at the *progressing* level across two or more settings. Student typically can: • Read basic texts with adult support. • Demonstrate an expanded sight vocabulary and phonological skills. • Use writing, typing, or other mediums to create simple short texts.	Student demonstrates a consistent understanding of the basic concepts and skills contained in the language arts items. He or she performs many of the skills in four or more language arts strands at the *progressing level* and some skills at the *accomplished* level in multiple settings. Student typically can: • Read basic texts with very limited or not support. • Make connections between information in a text and previously read materials or life experiences. • Write or type simple stories, journal entries, and letters with minimal support. • Answer appropriately to some comprehension questions.
Gr 6 0--------------------13	14------------------------53	54----------------------129	130--------------------204
Gr 7 0--------------------16	17------------------------59	60----------------------134	135--------------------204
Gr 8 0--------------------19	20------------------------64	65----------------------139	140--------------------204

FIGURE 5.2. MAAECF Language Arts Proficiency Level Score and Decision Summary. From Missouri Department of Education (2008); *www.mde.k12.ms.us/maaecf.*

in a recent, representative, and reliable manner. Geraldo's parents received a report summarizing his overall performance level scores for each content domain. Geraldo also was included in school and state accountability reports. The ultimate purpose of the MAAECF is to provide students with significant disabilities an opportunity to be included and participate in standards-based accountability and reform. For Geraldo, full inclusion in the MAAECF facilitated this process.

OTHER CHALLENGES
IN IMPLEMENTING ALTERNATE ASSESSMENTS

AA-AAS represent a relatively recent addition to most state's student assessment and accountability systems. Ongoing changes in federal and state regulations regarding alternate assessment demand innovation and flexibility on the part of educational leaders and classroom teachers to insure meaningful assessment results. A few prominent challenges are outlined in the sections that follow.

Defining Proficient Performance on AA-AAS

In May 2003, the U.S. Department of Education issued a proposed change in policy concerning NCLB and students with significant disabilities. This change to NCLB permitted states to develop alternate achievement standards for students with the most significant cognitive disabilities. These alternate achievement standards also must be aligned with the state's academic content standards and should reflect professional judgment of the highest learning standards possible for those students" (U.S. Department of Education, 2003, p. 4). This policy challenged educational leaders to define what "proficient performance" and "adequate yearly progress" should mean for students who take an AA-AAS.

To address this challenge, some states undertook standard setting procedures for their AA-AAS (Lewis, Mitzel, & Green, 1996; Roach & Elliott, 2004). Standard setting is the process of determining appropriate scores that correspond to a specified level of performance. The purpose is to establish "cut scores" that are based on what students in each performance level should know and be able to perform. For example, if a student obtained or exceeded the cut score corresponding to the "proficient" performance level, then that student should have demonstrated knowledge, skills, and competencies sufficient to be called "proficient." This requires educators to first specify what a student who achieves proficiency should understand and be able to do, and then to determine the AA-AAS score that corresponds to those expectations. In cases where states' AA-AAS utilized portfolio or performance assessments, other standard setting approaches might be utilized. For example, some states may utilized "body of work" approaches to standard setting, which involve compiling sets of evidence and student data (e.g., sample portfolios) that represent the range of possible performance levels from lowest to highest. Another possibility is a "reasoned judgment" approach to standard setting in which a group of experts determine the appropriate methods and indicators to use for categorizing student performance into different performance levels (Thompson, Johnstone, et al., 2005).

What is important to remember is that the most essential outcome of standard setting processes is not the scores associated with proficiency levels but the descriptions of what students who achieve the various performance levels typically know and are able to do. By examining the description of typical student performance in a given performance level, educators can gain an understanding of the knowledge, skills, and abilities typically held by students in that performance level and identify things that a given student is not yet able to perform consistently. This type of information helps teachers communicate with others about a student's progress, next year's instructional goals for the student, and the status of the student relative to the state's learning standards (Roach & Elliott, 2004).

Time and Timing

The issue of time and timing are challenges that are always a consideration in any assessment but are particularly relevant when implementing alternate assessments. The collection of recent, representative, and reliable learning evidence by teachers and others means that these assessments should be connected to and/or embedded within classroom instruction. Although some states do not formally require that a portfolio (or collection of student work) be assembled, most classroom teachers do collect work samples, teacher-made tests, and observations over several weeks time that then serve as the basis for evaluative judgments about student learning. In addition to the amount of time needed to collect and score information, educators must understand when they must report the AA-AAS results so that students' scores can be integrated with the test results of students participating in other assessments in the state accountability system. Thus, timing of the assessment can introduce a number of challenges to conducting an alternate assessment.

A survey of 206 teachers in Kentucky demonstrated another time-related issue with AA-AAS implementation. Survey respondents indicated the AA-AAS required between 25 to 35 hours outside of regular instructional time to complete (Kampfer, Horvath, Kleinert, & Kearns, 2001). Kampfer and colleagues's findings replicate previous survey research that indicated some teachers in Kentucky perceived the alternate assessment as taking time away from actual instruction (Kleinert, Kennedy, & Kearns, 1999). It appears Kentucky's Alternate Portfolio process may represent the upper end of the continuum of time allocation (e.g., preliminary case studies on the Idaho AA-AAS indicated teachers were spending between 2 and 4 hours per student assessed). However, because many special educators report concerns regarding large caseloads and inadequate time for planning and paperwork, any additional time commitments necessary to complete AA-AAS may undermine the acceptability and sustainability of the process (Avramidis & Norwich, 2002; Lipsky & Gartner, 1996; Roach, Elliott, & Berndt, 2007).

Access to the General Curriculum

One of the primary reasons for implementing AA-AAS is to ensure curriculum and instruction in the core academic areas (e.g., reading, mathematics, and science) are provided to students with the significant cognitive disabilities. Unfortunately, relatively little research exists on efforts to teach general academic content to this population. Nietupski, Harme-

Nietupski, Curtin, and Shrikanth (1997) reviewed 785 articles on the education of students with significant disabilities published from 1976 to 1995. Their review suggested less than 10% of the articles addressed academic skills and/or access to the general education curriculum (Browder & Cooper-Duffy, 2003). Similarly, Browder and Xin (1998) reviewed 48 studies on teaching sight words to students with significant disabilities, but only a few of these articles addressed reading instruction embedded in or connected to the instructional goals of the general education curriculum (Browder, Wakeman, Spooner, Ahlgrim-Delzell, & Algozzine, 2006). To support implementation of the AA-AAS process, states and school districts will need to provide additional training and resources to support teachers' efforts to provide access to the grade-level content standards for students with significant cognitive disabilities. Additional information on facilitating curricular access for students with disabilities, including students who participate in AA-AAS, is discussed in Chapter 6 of this book.

ALTERNATE ASSESSMENTS
BASED ON MODIFIED ACHIEVEMENT STANDARDS

In April 2007, the U.S. Department of Education again revised NCLB regulations to provide additional flexibility to states to facilitate the appropriate measurement of the achievement of certain students with disabilities. These revisions allowed states to develop AA-MAS. According the U.S. Department of Education Non-regulatory Guidance (2007), AA-MAS "are intended . . . for a limited group of students whose disability has prevented them from attaining grade-level proficiency" (p. 20). These new assessments are intended to support documentation of the performance of a small, but significant group of students with disabilities. The U.S. Department of Education has, therefore, capped the number of students who may demonstrate proficiency via AA-MAS at 2% of a state's or school district's students at a specific grade level.

The AA-MAS are intended to measure the same grade-level content as states' general assessments but will include less difficult items or item modifications (e.g., visual cues, fewer answer choices, key terms bolded) that are intended to make these tests more accessible. These new tests will be referenced to modified achievement standards developed by each state. A modified achievement standard is "an expectation of performance that is challenging . . . but may be less difficult than a grade-level academic achievement standard. Modified academic achievement standards must be aligned with a State's academic content standards for the grade in which a student is enrolled" (p. 14). It is important to note that these modified achievement standards are intended to be more challenging than states' alternate achievement standards, which may feature content that is simplified from and narrower in scope than the general grade-level standards.

Most states have only recently begun to develop their policies and strategies for AA-MAS; thus, it is difficult to know much about what these assessments will look like and which students will take them. According to the nonregulatory guidance (2007) document, the U.S. Department of Education has recommended the following sample criteria for student participation in AA-MAS:

1. There must be objective evidence demonstrating that the student's disability has precluded the student from achieving grade-level proficiency. Such evidence may include the student's performance on state assessments or other assessments that can validly document academic achievement.
2. The student's progress to date in response to appropriate instruction, including special education and related services designed to address the student's individual needs, is such that, even if significant growth occurs, the IEP Team is reasonably certain that the student will not achieve grade-level proficiency within the year covered by the student's IEP. The IEP Team must use multiple technically adequate measures of the student's progress over time in making this determination.
3. The student's IEP must include goals that are based on the academic content standards for the grade in which the student is enrolled (p. 17).

It is important to understand that AA-MAS are not intended to be out-of-level tests. Assessing students on a test intended for a different (often lower) grade level results in scores of questionable validity as well as discourages efforts to provide instruction referenced to grade-level content standards. In lieu of using out-of-level tests, states might implement the following strategies to develop their AA-MAS: (1) reducing the number of items on the general test; (2) eliminating the more difficult test items; (3) providing fewer answer choices on multiple-choice questions; or (4) providing visuals and graphics that support student understanding (Cortiella, 2007). As part of their efforts to develop AA-MAS processes, states and test developers will need to conduct evaluations to support the validity of scores resulting from these inclusive assessment strategies.

ALTERNATE ASSESSMENTS BASED ON GRADE-LEVEL ACHIEVEMENT STANDARDS

NCLB allows for a third type of alternate assessment, alternate assessments based on grade-level achievement standards (AA-GAS), for measuring the performance of students with disabilities. In the case of AA-GAS, states must demonstrate that student proficient performance on the alternate assessment is comparable (or equivalent) to proficiency demonstrated via the general large-scale assessment. It is important to understand that AA-GAS is a less common component of states' accountability systems; many states have not (and have no plans to) develop this form of assessment. Even in cases where this form of alternate assessment is in place (e.g., Massachusetts) relatively few students have been assessed using an AA-GAS (Wiener, 2006).

Wiener (2006) provided an overview of Massachusetts' development and implementation of an AA-GAS (also called the "competency portfolio"). Although the Massachusetts competency portfolio process can be used to include students' performance in NCLB-mandated reporting, Wiener identifies another compelling purpose for development of the state's AA-GAS: providing an alternate method of passing the state's graduation test, so that students can receive a high school diploma. When students with disabilities have met the other requirements (e.g., coursework, attendance) for receiving a diploma, but cannot passed the graduate exam with accommodation and multiple administrations,

> IEP teams [should] be permitted to designate these students for alternate assessments, when necessary, and . . . these students [should] be permitted to meet all state requirements to graduate when they take these alternate assessments. Taking an alternate assessment should not automatically remove any student from the possibility of earning a diploma, since in many cases it is not know precisely how much these students are capable of learning. (Wiener, 2006, p. 6)

The Massachusetts competency portfolio consists of a set of student-generated work samples in English/language arts and mathematics. Requirements for the portfolio components were developed by content area and assessment experts. An overview of these requirements are provided in Appendix 5.2. Although many states have not yet developed an AA-GAS, the introduction of graduation examinations that some students with disabilities will be unable to "pass" may compel additional states to explore adding this component to their accountability systems.

SUMMARY: ACHIEVING THE PROMISE
OF ALTERNATE ASSESSMENT

As stated in the *Standards for Educational and Psychological Testing*, "Tests are commonly administered in the expectation that some benefit will be realized from the intended use of scores.... A fundamental purpose of validation is to determine whether these specific benefits are likely to be realized" (American Educational Research Association, 1999, p. 16). Alternate assessments provide an opportunity for up to 3% of students in states, school districts, and schools (i.e., 1% on AA-AAS and 2% on AA-MAS) to demonstrate "proficient" performance in state-level accountability systems. Thus, alternate assessments can potentially help educators and educational systems show they are making adequate progress toward the goal of having all students "proficient" on statewide assessments. This is an important potential outcome because the performance of many students with disabilities has traditionally been excluded for the evaluation of instructional improvement and reform efforts. In addition, alternate assessments are intended to facilitate inclusion and motivate special educators to provide standards-based curriculum and instruction to students with disabilities. As state's AA-AAS, AA-MAS, and (in some cases) AA-GAS systems are fully developed and implemented, careful consideration of assessment results at both the student and system levels will provide compelling evidence regarding our progress toward recognizing these goals.

Language Arts ~Grades 6–8 ~ Evidence Worksheets

MSIS ID Number ☐☐☐☐☐☐☐☐

Grade ☐   District Code ☐☐☐

	Cluster 1 C. Reading Words and Sentences (Place a check mark by the appropriate evidence sources.)	Work Samples /Tests	Obser-vations	Media Recorded	Interviews
8	Student recognizes and reads basic sight words.				
9	Student reads and recognizes names of classmates, family members, and teachers.				
10	Student matches print words to objects.				
11	Student reads printed words.				
12	Student reads simple sentences fluently.				

*Each MAA item cluster must be documented with a minimum of **two sources** (work samples/tests, observations, media recorded, interviews), and each source must be accompanied by **at least one piece of evidence documented on the appropriate Evidence Worksheets**.

W o r k   S a m p l e s / T e s t s

Evidence Source (Check Type of Source)	**Overall Description of Performance**
☐ Student Work Samples ☐ Teacher-made Tests ☐ Norm Referenced Tests ☐ Other:_____	*Tasks or Activities:* *Student Response(s):* *Support Needed:* *Number of Settings:*

LA 6-8 1.C

Date(s) of Samples or Tests	Comments on Performance for Specific Samples of Behavior

January 2008   Copyright © 2008 Mississippi Department of Education

O b s e r v a t i o n s

Instructions: Observe one to three separate times, indicate the date and document exactly what was observed.

Comments on performance: Note the level of student independence and the number of different settings in which the skill occurs.

Student's Task:			
Observation 1 Date: _____	**Teacher Stimuli:** **Setting:** **Support:**	**Student Response:**	**If Multiple Trials, please complete:** **Number of Trials:** **Number Correct:** **Average Support Needed:**
Observation 2 Date: _____	**Teacher Stimuli:** **Setting:** **Support:**	**Student Response:**	**If Multiple Trials, please complete:** **Number of Trials:** **Number Correct:** **Average Support Needed:**
Observation 3 Date: _____	**Teacher Stimuli:** **Setting:** **Support:**	**Student Response:**	**If Multiple Trials, please complete:** **Number of Trials:** **Number Correct:** **Average Support Needed:**
Summary of Observation: (Needed support, setting, etc.)			

98

Media Recorded(Video/Photo/Audio)

Instructions: Document one to three separate occasions. Indicate the date and document exactly what was recorded. Please attach additional photos on a blank sheet if more space is need. Submit actual video or audio tape along with this evidence sheet.

Comments on performance: Describe the task the student was engaged in, the degree of accuracy with which he/she responded, the level of support needed, and the number of different settings in which the skill occurred.

Attach photos in space above.

I n t e r v i e w s

Date(s) of Interview(s): _____ _____ _____ _____

Interview Questions Relevant to Target Skill(s) Being Assessed:
_____
_____
_____
_____

Name of Interviewee: _____ **Instructional Role:** _____

Interviewee's description of tasks or activities in which the student exhibits the targeted skill:

Interviewee's description of how well the skill is performed:

Interviewee's description of support needed to perform the skill:

Interviewee's description of the setting(s) where the skill is exhibited:

MCAS-Alt Grade 10 "Competency Portfolio" Requirements in ELA and Math

Following are the specific MCAS-Alt portfolio requirements for a student in grade 10 (or beyond) to earn a *Competency Determination:*

The student's portfolio must:
1. demonstrate knowledge and skills *at grade-level expectations for a student in grade 10*;
2. reflect a performance level of *needs improvement* or higher in both ELA and Mathematics; and
3. document that the student has independently addressed *all* required learning standards and strands in the subject being assessed, as described below.

ENGLISH LANGUAGE ARTS (ELA)—portfolios must reflect the learning standards in the Massachusetts *English Language Arts Curriculum Framework* (June 2001) and must include:

- **FIVE written work samples** as described below;
- **Multiple drafts** of each work sample that indicate a progression of the student's thinking in each successive draft. Each must:
  —be clearly identified on the first page with a title, the student's name, and the date on which it was produced;
  —be written in the words of the student, with independent edits and meaningful revisions incorporated into subsequent drafts (i.e., not rewritten by the teacher for the student);
  —include a clear description of the type(s) and frequency of assistance provided to the student by the teacher; and
  —not include worksheets, short-answer tests, quizzes, or plot summaries.

An English language arts portfolio may include evidence produced and accumulated over **more than one school year**, beginning as early as grade 9. Evidence may be added to a previously submitted portfolio, or replaced with higher-quality work, and the entire portfolio resubmitted each year beyond grade 10 until the student demonstrates a level of performance equivalent to that of a student who scored *needs improvement* or higher on the grade 10 ELA MCAS test.

English Language Arts Strand:	A grade 10 portfolio *must* include the following components, at minimum, in order to be considered for the *Competency Determination*.
Language	Evidence, provided either in separate work samples or incorporated into the five required writing samples, that the student understands and is independently able to analyze and appropriately apply the following: • **Vocabulary:** words used correctly; literal/figurative meaning • **Grammar and usage:** sentence structure and language conventions • **Mechanics:** punctuation and spelling
Reading and Literature	**Three essays or compositions, including all drafts, and based on grade 10 literature** in which the student analyzes, interprets, compares and contrasts, and/or discusses the meaning of the following: 1. a work of **literary nonfiction,** 2. a work of **fiction,** and 3. a work of either **poetry** or **drama.**

(continued)

From Wiener (2006).

Composition	**Two essays or compositions, including all drafts,** that demonstrate original thinking and independent editing through several drafts, as follows: 1. **one essay or composition** in which the student identifies and discusses a theme in literature appropriate to a student in grade 10 and/or connects such a literary theme to his or her life 2. **one essay or composition**, including all drafts, on a topic of the student's own choosing that is reflective, persuasive, or fictional

MATHEMATICS—Mathematics portfolios must reflect the learning standards in the most recent Massachusetts *Mathematics Curriculum Framework* (November 2000) and must include:

- a **table of contents** listing each piece of evidence (work sample) submitted, and the strand and learning standard(s) it purports to address,
- at least **four examples or problems** solved correctly by the student that demonstrate all aspects of each learning standard documented in the portfolio. Additional examples of each standard are strongly encouraged. Original evidence, rather than photocopies, is preferred,
- a *Grade 10 Work Description* attached to each work sample that documents a particular learning standard,
- a **score** (% accurate) given by the teacher for each work sample,
- work samples produced as independently as possible by the student; corrections made by the teacher may not be submitted as the student's own work,
- written evidence of the student's thinking and problem-solving, indicating the process used to solve each problem (i.e., "show all work"),
- a clear indication of the type(s) and frequency of assistance provided to the student by the teacher, either written directly on each piece or described on the *Grade 10 Work Description*.

Students in grade 10 may not have had an opportunity to take all mathematics courses needed to satisfy the requirements listed below. Therefore, a Mathematics portfolio may include evidence produced over a period of **more than one school year**, beginning not earlier than grade 9. Evidence may be added to an existing portfolio and resubmitted annually beyond grade 10.

Mathematic Strand:	A grade 10 portfolio *must* include evidence that addresses at least the following learning standards to be considered for the *Competency Determination:*
Number Sense and Operations	*A total of at least* two *work samples, one documenting each of the two learning standards listed below:* 10.N.1—Identify and use the propertie of operations on real numbers, Including the associative, commutative, and distributive properties [do not simply define these properties: show how they are applied and demonstrate that students can identify each property; e.g., usse the distributive property to multiply $7(23) = 7(20 + 3) = 7(20) + 7(3) = 140 + 21 = 161$]; the existence of the identity and inverse elements for addition and multiplicatlon: the existence of nth root of positive real numbers for any positive integer n: and the inverse relationship between taking the nth root of and the nth power of a positive real number. 10.N.2—Simplify numerical expressions, including those involving positive integer exponents or the absolute value [e.g., $3(2^4 - 1) = 45, 4|3 - 5| + 6 = 14$]; apply such simplifications in the solution of problems.

(continued)

Patterns, Relation, and Algebra	*A total of at least* four *work samples, one documenting each of the four learning standards listed below;* 10.P.2—Demonstrate an understanding of the relationship between various representations of a line, Determine a line's slope and x- and y-intercept from its graph or from a linear equation that represents the line. Find a linear equation describing a line from a graph or a geometric description of the line (e.g., by using the "point-slope" or "slope y-intercept" formulas). Explain the significance of a positive, negative, zero, or undefined slope. 10.P.4—Demonstrate facility in symbolic manipulation of polynomial and rational expressions by rearranging and collecting terms; factoring [e.g., $a^2 - b^2 = (a + b)(a - b)$; $x^2 + 10x + 21 = (x + 3)(x + 7)$; $5x^4 + 10x^3 - 5x^2 = 5x^2(x^2 + 2x - 1)$]; identifying and canceling common factors in rational expressions; and applying the properties of positive integer exponents. [This standard does *not* include simple addition, subtraction, and multiplication of polynomials, as covered in 10.P.3.] 10.P.5—Find solution to quadratic equations (with real roots) by factoring, completing the square, or using the quadratic formula, Demonstrate an understanding of the equivalence of the methods. 10.P.7—Solve everyday problems that can be modeled using linear, reciprocal, quadratic, or exponential functions, Apply appropriate tabular, graphical, or symbolic methods to the solution. Include compound interest and direct and inverse variation problems, Use technology when appropriate.
Geometry	*A total of at least* three *work samples, one documenting each* any three learning standards *listed below:* 10.G.1—Identify figures using properties of sides, angles, and diagonals. Identify the figure and type(s) of symmetry. 10.G.2—Draw congruent and similar figures using a compass, straightedge, protractor, and other tools such as computer software, Make conjectures about method of construction. Justify the conjecture by logical arguments. 10.G.3—Recognize and solve problems involving angles formed by transversals of coplanar lines. Identify and determine the measure of central and inscribed angles and their associated minor and major arcs. Recognize and solve problems associated with radii, chords, and arc within or on the same circle. 10.G.4—Apply congruence and similarity correspondences (e.g. $\triangle ABC \cong \triangle XYZ$) and properties of the figure to find missing parts of geometric figures, and provide logical justification. 10.G.5—Solve simple triangle problems using the triangle angle sum property and Pythagorean theorem. 10.G.6—Use the properties of special triangles (e.g., isosceles, equilateral, 30°–60°–90°; 45°–45°–90°) to solve problems. 10.G.7—Using rectangular coordinates, calculate midpoints of segments, slopes of line and segments, and distances between two points, and apply the results to the solutions of problems. 10.G.8–Find linear equations that represent lines either perpendicular or parallel to a given line and through a point, e.g., by using the "point-slope" form of the equation.

(continued)

	10.G.9—Draw the results, and interpret transformations on figures in the coordinate plane, e.g., translations, reflections, rotations, scale factors, and the results of successive transformations. Apply transformations to the solutions of problems. 10.G.10—Demonstrate the ability to visualize solid objects and recognize projections and cross sections. 10.G.11—Use vertex-edge graphs to model and solve problems (i.e., network).
Measurement	*A total of at least* three *work samples, one documenting each of the three learning standards listed below:* 10.M.1—Calculate perimeter, circumference, and area of common geometric figures such as parallelograms, trapezoids, circles, and triangles. 10.M.2—Given the formula, find the lateral area, surface area, and volume of prisms, pyramids, spheres, cylinders, and cones (e.g., find the volume of a sphere with a specified surface area). 10.M.3—Relate changes in the measurement of one attribute of an object to changes in other attributes, e.g., how changing radius or height of a cylinder affects its surface area or volume
Data Analysis, Statistics, and Probability	*A total of at least* two *work samples, one documenting each of the two learning standards listed below:* 10.D.1—Select, create, and interpret an appropriate graphical representation (e.g., scarterplot, table, stem-and-leaf plot, box-and-whisker plot, circle graph, line graph, line plot) for a set of data and use appropriate statistics (e.g., mean, median, range, mode) to communicate information about the data. Use these notions to compare different sets of data. 10.D.2—Approximate a line of best fit (i.e., draw a trend line) given a set of data (e.g., scatterplot). Use technology when appropriate.

6

Facilitating and Evaluating Access to the General Education Curriculum

IDEA 2004 is explicit that *all* students receive instruction that allow them to make progress toward state and district academic standards: "Almost 30 years of research and experience has demonstrated that the education of students with disabilities can be made more effective by having high expectations for such children and insuring their access to the general education curriculum in the regular classroom, to the maximum extent possible" (20 U.S.C. § 140(c)(5)(A). NCLB has reinforced this expectation by requiring that *all* students demonstrate proficiency on state academic achievement standards by 2013–2014. As outlined in previous chapters in this book, students with disabilities may demonstrate proficiency in a variety of ways: participation in general large-scale assessments with or without testing accommodations, alternate assessments based on modified achievement standards, or alternate assessments based on alternate achievement standards. Similarly, students who are ELLs may demonstrate their proficiency using testing accommodations or alternate forms of assessment.

Development and implementation of inclusive assessment strategies mandated by NCLB, however, can be considered only one element of our efforts to improve achievement for students with disabilities. If students with disabilities and ELLs are not afforded the same (or perhaps) greater opportunities to learn the skills and concepts on standards-focused assessments, they can easily become scapegoats for the inability of schools, districts, and states to reach NCLB's mandates for AYP. "During the past half-century there has been a growing body of evidence supporting a fundamental educational truism: that *what* and *how much* students are taught is associated with, and likely influences, *what* and *how much* they learn" (Anderson, 2002, p. 255). This would appear especially true for students with disabilities and ELLs who often require intensive, explicit instruction to master new skills and concepts. For many of these students, "teaching to the test" by explicitly including skills and knowledge from the state standards in their instructional experiences is an essential step in providing access in the general curriculum (Browder, Fallin, et al., 2003).

This chapter begins with an overview of federal regulations that address access to the general curriculum. Curricular access also is defined and located within a variety of approaches to curriculum for students with disabilities. Finally, to support readers' work with students with disabilities and ELL, we provide an overview of different frameworks for facilitating access to the general curriculum.

ACCESS TO THE GENERAL CURRICULUM AND OPPORTUNITY TO LEARN IN FEDERAL REGULATIONS AND GUIDELINES

Federal guidance regarding AA-MAS and AA-AAS presume students access the general curriculum. The U.S. Department of Education nonregulatory guidance document for AA-MAS stated "(a) State's guidelines must ensure that a student who is assessed based on modified academic achievement standards has access to the curriculum, including instruction, for the grade in which the student is enrolled" (§200.1(f)(2)(iii)) (2007). Similarly, the nonregulatory guidance document for AA-AAS indicated "alternate achievement standards must be aligned with a State's academic content standards, promote access to the general curriculum, and reflect professional judgment of the highest achievement standards possible" (See 34 C.F.R. §200.1(d)) (U.S. Department of Education, 2005). Thus, for *all* students (including those students with the most significant cognitive disabilities) access to the general education curriculum is an important educational objective.

Access to the general curriculum can be considered connected to another educational concept: opportunity to learn. Opportunity to learn (OTL) "operationalizes what is taking place in schools and classrooms to support students' learning and progress, particularly relative to new expectations for student performance" (Herman, Klein, & Abedi, 2000, p. 16). OTL standards originally were proposed in 1992 report of the National Council on Educational Standards and Testing. The proposal met with political opposition, however, and OTL standards were made "voluntary" in *Goals 2000* and the reauthorization of ESEA (U.S. Department of Education, 1994). *Goals 2000* defined OTL standards as "the criteria for, and the basis of assessing the sufficiency or quality of the resources, practices, and conditions necessary at each level of the education system to provide all students with the opportunity to learn the material in voluntary national content standards or state content standards" (§3[a][7]). These voluntary OTL standards (§213[c][2]) were intended to insure the quality of various components of the educational system, including:

- Curricula and instructional materials (including media and other technology).
- Teacher knowledge, education, and skill.
- The availability and quality of professional development.
- Alignment of curriculum (i.e., content standards), classroom instruction, and assessments.
- School and classroom discipline and safety (Ysseldyke, Thurlow, & Shin, 1995).

Although proponents of OTL standards believed they were essential for achieving equity and understanding the effectiveness of curricular and instructional changes, they have not been codified into subsequent iterations of standards-based reform and accountability (e.g., NCLB). Close consideration of the meaning of access to the general education curriculum, however, illustrates the close relationship between the two concepts. By taking a "broad lens" to our efforts to define and facilitate curricular access, educators can make significant progress toward recognizing the promise of OTL.

DEFINING THE GENERAL EDUCATION CURRICULUM

The *general education curriculum* is a blanket term that refers to multiple components of the educational system. Nolet and McLaughlin (2000) suggested the general education curriculum "includes the full range of courses, activities, lessons, and materials used routinely by the general population of the school" (p. 29). Clearly, state and district-level academic content standards are among the most prominent framework for understanding the general education curriculum. This is sometimes referred to as the *intended curriculum*; that is, this is the official sanctioned set of goals and objectives that educational leaders and community members hope students will learn. It is important to note that students' IEPs are not meant to serve as the intended curriculum; "the IEP is a plan for making the intended curriculum more immediate and specific for student" (Nolet & McLaughlin, p. 16).

As some researchers have illustrated (e.g., Spillane, 1999), the *intended curriculum* expressed in academic content standards is not the only form of curriculum that exists in educational systems. Facilitating curricular access requires being aware of and evaluating the *taught curriculum* (i.e., the daily and ongoing content of teachers' instruction) and the *learned curriculum* (i.e., the actual skills and concepts learned by students). Unfortunately, for a variety of reasons, the content of these three curricula (intended, taught, and learned) do not agree consistently, resulting in less effective teaching and diminished student outcomes.

In order to facilitate access for students with disabilities and ELLs, educators need to go beyond the content standards to consider other components of general education curriculum and instruction. Hitchcock, Meyer, Rose, and Jackson (2002) identify four main components of the general education curriculum:

1. Goals and milestones for instruction (often in the form of a scope and sequence document);
2. Media and materials used by students;
3. Specific instructional methods (often described in a teacher's edition); and
4. Means of assessment to measure student progress (pp. 3–4).

As students progress through the grade levels, textbooks increasingly dominate the curricula and structure the instructional approaches in the general education classrooms. The overreliance on textbooks to anchor learning creates a variety of barriers to access and involvement for students with disabilities and ELLs. Clearly, a major barrier is the reading level of the written texts. If students with disabilities and ELL cannot decode and comprehend the textbook, access and involvement in the general education curriculum and classroom instruction can be compromised. Even when students can decode the text, the reading and linguistic "load" can be overwhelming, making it difficult for students to read and retain information from multiple pages, sections, or chapters. Another difficulty is that features of the textbooks often do not support students' understanding; for example, pictures and graphics may not illustrate the ideas and content outlined in the accompanying text. Although some textbook publishers are developing audio or computer-based versions of the text, much work remains to bring universal design for learning (UDL) features to texts used in most classrooms (see Chapter 7 for a discussion of UDL). As Hitchcock and colleagues (2002) stated, "These materials are rarely core and tend to be seen as enhancements. They represent 'add-ons' rather than true alternative ways of presenting essential concepts" (p. 10). As it stands, the centrality of the textbook in most general education classrooms is a serious barrier to access.

General educators' choice of instructional and evaluative methods also can create an additional barrier to access to the general curriculum for ELLs and students with disabilities. Many general education classroom teachers primarily rely on verbal and visual presentation of material to large groups of students (usually whole-class instruction). Lectures often are followed by teacher-led discussions of the concepts presented or independent seat work with students reading to themselves and composing answers or responses. Research suggests (Cazden, 1988; Mehan, 1979) initiation–response–evaluation (or IRE) methods are the primary mode of interpersonal interaction typically used in classroom discussions. In IRE,

> Teachers ask innumerable questions to which the answers are already preestablished. Students are drawn into a pattern of guessing the answer that teacher already had in mind when he or she ask the question. Finally, students' answers to the questions tend to be brief in nature, including simple "yes" or "no" responses. (Baxter, Woodward, Voorhies, & Wong, 2002, p. 173)

For students with disabilities and ELLs, IRE methods are unlikely to facilitate and support the types of higher-order thinking and comprehension of complex concepts demanded by the general education curriculum.

Small group instruction, multiple presentation and response modalities, and collaboration with peers may be needed to provide students with disabilities and ELLs access to the materials and instruction in the general education classroom. Teacher-developed assessments (and tests provided as support materials of the textbook series) often measure aspects of students' disabilities or LEP. For example, although a mathematics test may include concepts and skills understood by students with disabilities and ELLs, it may feature questions and directions to these students that cannot be read. In these cases, the reading expectations of the test may hinder the student's ability to demonstrate his or her mathematics achievement. It is important that educators understand how to select and implement testing accommodations (see Chapter 3) in their classrooms in order to support students' access and success with the assessment component of the general education curriculum.

SPECIAL EDUCATION AND MODELS OF CURRICULUM

The emphasis on attaining academic achievement represents a dramatic departure from the curriculum and inclusion practices that traditionally have been implemented with many students with disabilities. The initial passage of Public Law 94-142 was a transformative moment in the education of children with disabilities. This legislation literally "opened the doors" of public schools for many students who had been denied access to educational services because their disabilities were viewed as insurmountable impediments to learning (Hitchcock et al., 2002).

Public Law 94-142 ensured access to a free and appropriate education for students with disabilities, but "simple access to an individualized education proved an insufficient foundation for success" (Hitchcock et al., 2002, p. 3). Early attempts at special education embraced a "developmental model" for students with significant disabilities that featured curriculum and instruction deemed "appropriate" for students' assessment-derived mental ages. Student with disabilities often received a relatively narrow curriculum that focused on age-inappropriate concepts and skills (e.g., stacking blocks, stringing beads). Other students with disabilities were provided with ongoing remediation of basic literacy and mathematics skills (often in pull-out or self-contained classrooms) at the expense of their exposure and participation in the general education curriculum.

In the 1970s and 1980s, special educators began to use the "criterion of ultimate functioning" to design functional curricula that addressed students' self-care, social, and vocational needs. Special education services were refocused to address skills and concepts students would need for independent living in the community and successful functioning in the workplace. "It was not unusual to see IEP objectives such as 'checking out a book from the library,' 'eating lunch in the school cafeteria,' and 'packaging equipment at a hospital job site'" (Ford et al., 2001, p. 214). Although functional curricula, community-based instruction, and vocational education represented progress in terms of their utility and age appropriateness for students with disabilities, this approach generally did not result in greater access to general education classrooms and instruction.

Over the past few decades, educators and family members have begun to develop and implement tactics to promote the inclusion of students with disabilities in general education settings. Early considerations of mainstreaming and least restrictive environment (LRE) generally focused on the socialization and self-esteem benefits for students with disabilities as well as increased tolerance and understanding on the part of students without disabilities. More recent practices have maintained the focus on relationships and self-concept but have added an emphasis on exposure to the general curriculum and the broader school experience (Ford et al., 2001). Creating inclusive educational contexts has served as an important first step in facilitating access to and success with the general education curriculum. Through early efforts at inclusion and mainstreaming, special and general educators began to explore and understand various strategies for supporting and facilitating the success of students with disabilities in general education contexts (Roach & Elliott, 2006).

NCLB and (to a lesser extent) IDEA 2004 have redefined access to the general education curriculum. Although each student with disabilities will continue to have the legal right to individualize instructional curricular and supports, progress toward achievement in the general education curriculum has become the optimal target. As a result, physical presence in inclusive settings does not meet the spirit of these laws, instead students with disabilities must have instruction and accommodations that promote their learning of the content and skills outlined in grade-level content standards (Pugach & Warger, 2001; Roach & Elliott, 2006).

Some of the difficulties that confront, and misconceptions that derail, educators' facilitation of access to the general education curriculum for students with disabilities were illuminated by a recent survey of 200 special educators who work with students with significant disabilities (Agran, Alper, & Wehmeyer, 2002). A majority of respondents (53%) reported their school district had no plan in place to support access to the general curriculum by students with significant disabilities. In addition, many teachers suggested addressing grooming, social skills, communication, choice making, and problem solving were more important than ensuring students' access to and progress in the general education curriculum. Survey respondents also indicated that challenging behavior and resistance from general educators and administrators were significant barriers to facilitating students' access to the general curriculum. As Agran et al. lamented, "Most distressingly, (these findings) will deny access to the general curriculum for a number of students. Rather than develop creative and sound support systems for students, placement decisions may instead focus on whether the student is "ready for" or can "earn" his or her way into general education" (p. 131).

IEPS AND ACCESS TO THE GENERAL CURRICULUM

In its requirements for students' IEPs, IDEA 2004 clearly mandates that students with disabilities should have access to the general education curriculum and academic standards. Specifically, students' IEPs must include consideration of how the student will access the general education curriculum. Specifically, each student's IEPs must address (1) how his or her present level of performance and disability influence participation in the general education curriculum; (2) goals and objectives designed to facilitate his or her access to the general education curriculum; and (3) descriptions of the program modification and special services that will be provided to support the student's access and progress in the general education curriculum.

Karger (2004) posited "the IEP can be viewed as the central mechanism, both legally and educationally, for ensuring access to the general education curriculum" (p. 6). This centrality of the IEP document and process, however, places great responsibility on each member of the IEP team to consider how to facilitate each student's access to the general education classroom, involvement with general education instructional materials and activities, and progress toward meeting the expectations outlined in the general education content standards (Hitchcock et al., 2002).

Unfortunately, research suggests that the current IEP process does not result consistently in improved access and involvement in general education curriculum. In their case studies of students with significant disabilities, Fisher and Frey (2001) discovered a "disconnect" between students' IEPs and the curriculum and instruction provided in general education classrooms. Teachers and family members reported that the goals and objectives included in students' IEPs did not match the curriculum and instruction provided to students in inclusive environments. Fisher and Fry's findings are consistent with other research on IEPs that found minimal coordination between special educators and general educators (Lipsky & Gartner, 1997) and difficulties developing measurable goals and objectives for student progress in the general education curriculum (Yell, 1998).

A survey by the National Association of State Directors of Special Education (1999) of state-level administrators ($n = 33$) identified numerous difficulties in using students' IEPs as tools for facilitating access to the general curriculum. According to survey respondents:

1. IEP goals and objectives tended to address to reading and mathematics, but not other subject domains (e.g., social studies, science).
2. State content standards were viewed as too broad and complex to serve as a focus for students' IEP goals and objectives.
3. Parents and teachers needed additional information and training on how state standards apply to *all* students.
4. Special and general educators needed need professional development on how to link IEP goals and objectives to state content standards, large-scale assessments, and general curriculum materials.
5. Special and general educators needed access to and professional development on curriculum-based assessments for tracking students' progress on IEP goals and objectives that are linked to the general curriculum (Karger, 2004).

For the IEP to serve as the primary means for ensuring access to the general curriculum, states and school districts would need to provide extensive professional development and increased monitoring to ensure that the goals and support services outlined in IEP documents were implemented as planned. In short, the IDEA 2004 requirement for educators to address general education content standards in students' IEP documents represents a promising, but insufficient strategy for facilitating access.

FACILITATING ACCESS TO THE GENERAL CURRICULUM

To facilitate students' progress in meeting the expectations outlined in state content standards and measured on large scale assessments, general and special educators need access to and proficiency in using strategies and materials that support access to the general education curriculum. A variety of models and strategies have been proposed to support this work. This chapter provides an overview of some of these models and links to additional web-based resources are presented throughout the chapter.

Morocco (2001) provided an overview of the conceptual framework employed by the REACH Institute, a federally funded center to investigate instructional strategies that support students with disabilities in accessing and understanding the general education curriculum. The goal of the REACH Institute is to refocus teachers' efforts toward deeper conceptual understanding and experience with domain-specific modes of understanding (e.g., scientific method) rather from providing broad, but shallow exposure to the general education curriculum.

The REACH Institute's work focuses on creating instructional opportunities that include (1) authentic tasks, (2) use of cognitive strategies, (3) social mediation, and (4) constructive conversations. Authentic instructional tasks involve students in constructing, composing, and creating products. These tasks utilize student background knowledge and provide input and response options that honor different learning modalities: Media such as photographs, video, visual art, music, or PowerPoint presentation can be utilized in these tasks. "By the middle grades, students with disabilities have usually experienced debilitating failure in school and need tasks that are meaningful to their lives beyond school" (Morocco, 2001, p. 7) Therefore, the REACH Institute also recommends activities have applications to the world outside the classroom walls. Cognitive strategies that support student understanding are another important component of the REACH Institute's work. Strategy instruction in this model combines explicit teaching of general learning strategies with domain-specific ways of investigation and communicating results (e.g., creating a timeline in history).

The REACH Institute's work also focuses on the social supports and interactions that can facilitate access and understanding of the general education curriculum. Instructional activities are designed to encourage social mediation of student learning including (1) shared responsibility among groups of students for completing the tasks; (2) opportunities for students to share and explain there thinking; (3) tasks that call for multiple perspectives and allow more than one correct response; and (4) teacher support and modeling of peer interaction. To that end, the REACH Institute's work all emphasizes opportunities for constructive conversations.

> An extensive line of research has identified the characteristics of instructional conversations that build understanding, including opportunities for students to initiate the conversation and pose their own questions, the responsivity of the teacher to the content of students' comments, the opportunity for extended discourse on one topic, and the consistent focus on a theme (Goldenberg, 1992–1993). (Morocco, 2001, p. 9)

Direct instruction, teacher modeling, and constructive feedback is necessary to create a space for these sorts of conversations. In particular, students with disabilities may need guidance to develop question posing skills and to maintain focus on the concepts and ideas being discussed.

The REACH Institute's evaluation of this instructional model indicated students with disabilities made similar gains in skills and knowledge to their peers without disabilities. In addition, students with disabilities benefited from explicit instruction in domain-specific cognitive strategies. To support implementation of these conceptually rich instructional experiences, teachers needed ongoing comprehensive professional development opportunities. Moreover, the REACH Institute's evaluation suggested the need for continually progress monitoring and probing for student understanding via a diversity of assessment methods (e.g., journals, interviews, constructed response assessment items).

King-Sears (2001) outlined a three-step process for promoting access to the general education curriculum. This process begins with an analysis of the general education curriculum's goals, materials, and instructional supports. King-Sears provided the following three questions (p. 68) to structure this evaluation:

1. How well does the curriculum describe what learners should be able to know and do by the end of the course?
2. What resources are included in the curriculum that provide teachers with materials and research-based methods for diversifying instruction?
3. How many universal design elements are included in the curriculum?

It is important that special education teachers (and other support personnel such as school psychologists and counselors) become familiar with state grade-level content standards. By evaluating the goals and objectives included in the standards, educators can determine concepts and skills that will require specific support for students with disabilities (or ELLs). In addition, this sort of review can help special educators align what happens in individualized support sessions with the themes and concepts being addressed in the general education curriculum (King-Sears, 2001). In evaluating curricular materials, educators need to consider the research support for the instructional strategies included in teacher guides and other support materials. Curriculum developers should provide an overview of the empirical evidence that supports and demonstrates the effectiveness of curriculum and instructional materials. In addition, educators should be familiar with available databases of research-based educational practices, including:

- The What Works Clearinghouse (*ies.ed.gov/ncee/wwc*).
- *Practice Alerts* from the Council for Exception Children (*www.cecdr.org/subpage. cfm?id=DEA7864A-C09F-1D6F-F9008ABF5B1B71B1*).
- Task Force for Evidence-Based Interventions in School Psychology (*www.sp-ebi. org/index.html*).

Additional information on the universal design elements is presented in Chapter 7.

According to King-Sears's (2001) model, the second step in facilitating access to the general curriculum involves curricular enhancements. "Just because a particular general education curriculum is not well designed for learners with disabilities does *not* mean that the curriculum content is inaccessible. However, it does mean that teachers need to enhance certain features to make the content more accessible" (p. 70). To do this, King-Sears suggested teachers address a set of curriculum design elements identified by Simmons and Kame'enui (1996) as reasonable targets for curricular enhancements.

- Identify, define, and explicitly teach *big ideas* such as key vocabulary and themes, important events, connections between concepts.
- Provide explicit instruction, modeling, and on going support and feedback on the use of *strategies*. For example, students with disabilities may benefit from step-by-

step directions, visual cues regarding problem solving procedures, or instruction on effective study skills.

- Create a context for *mediated scaffolding*, including conversations between teachers and students, ample prompting, and questioning that leads students toward more sophisticated understanding of concepts.
- Teachers practice *strategic integration* and *judicious review* to connect new concepts and skills with previously learned concepts, and facilitate students' deeper understanding of curricular themes.
- *Primed background knowledge*, including attempts to connect curriculum to students' background knowledge and personal interests.

Addressing these curriculum designed features can help teachers make the general education curriculum more accessible to students with disabilities and ELLs.

The final component of King-Sears's (2001) model for creating access to the general education curriculum involves providing accommodations or modifications to instructional strategies and curricular materials. King-Sears outlines a four-tier approach to making these changes: accommodations, adaptations, parallel curriculum outcomes, and overlapping curricula. Additional information about each of these strategies is provided in Table 6.1. Educators should make efforts to begin their instructional planning with accommodation and adaptation; for students with more significant disabilities, parallel and overlapping curricula may be employed to meet their individualized educational needs within the general education classroom and curriculum.

Wehmeyer (2003) presents a similar model for providing curricular access to students with disabilities that includes three levels of modifications.

1. Curriculum adaptation: Modifying the representation or presentation of the general curriculum, or modifying the student's engagement with the general curriculum, to enhance progress.
2. Curriculum augmentation: Enhancing the general curriculum with learning strategies that support acquisition and generalization of skills and concepts (e.g., self-regulation skills, self-management, and mnemonics).
3. Curriculum alteration: Changing the general curriculum by adding content specific to students' needs, including self-care, vocational, and functional living skills.

Wehmeyer suggests planning for curricular access can be facilitated by working through the levels of curricular modifications in sequence. Unfortunately, research suggests that, in the case of students with moderate to severe disabilities, "the third level of curriculum modification (e.g., alternative curriculum) is where planning currently begins" (Wehmeyer, Lance, & Bashinski, 2002, p. 227). In Wehmeyer (2003), middle school students with disabilities received curriculum adaptations in only 2.78% of the intervals in which they were observed. To provide support for curricular access, Wehmeyer et al. (2002) has developed a flowchart (see Figure 6.1) that can be used by IEP teams determine which curricular modifications (if any) are needed to support students' access to the general education curriculum.

TABLE 6.1. Potential Changes to General Education Curriculum to Provide Access

Definition	Examples
Curricular Accommodations	
Content and conceptual/task complexity matches what is provided to other students, but variations in instructional delivery or student response facilitate access to general education curriculum.	• Student uses audio or computer-presented versions of textbooks. • Student is provided with graphic organizer and pictorial supports to facilitate understanding teacher lecture. • Student receives extra time to produce a written response to a writing prompt.
Curricular Adaptations	
Content matches what is provided to other students, but student is responsible for fewer or less complex ideas and concepts.	• Student memorizes 10 vocabulary terms in social studies rather than the 20 assigned to the rest of the class. • While the class works on multidigit subtractions with regrouping, student works on multidigit subtraction without regrouping.
Parallel Curricula	
Content is similar to what is provided to other students, but student is responsible for significantly less difficult concepts and/ or many fewer tasks and terms.	• While class is working on writing essays analyzing a piece of historical fiction, student writes a short description of a main character in the novel. • During class on human anatomy, student works on labeling the major organs in the body.
Overlapping Curricula	
Activities allow for engagement with general education curriculum and peers, but content, tasks, and expectations and outcomes are very different from what is expected other students.	• When cooperating with his/her lab partners on a science experiment, the student is working on IEP goals regarding (a) using materials safely and (b) using words to express his/her wants and needs.

SPECIALLY DESIGNED ACADEMIC INSTRUCTION IN ENGLISH

Specially Designed Academic Instruction in English (SDAIE) is used by teachers of ELLs to provide instruction in the general education curriculum when instruction in students' primary language is not available. SDAIE "combines second language acquisition principles with those elements of quality teaching that make a lesson understandable.... Such instruction enables [ELLs] to improve listening, speaking, reading, and writing through the study of an academic subject" (Diaz-Rico & Weed, 2002). It is important to note that in SDAIE the content of instruction remains the same as in other general education classrooms, but the instructional strategies and supports are varied in order to facilitate students' understanding of concepts and skills.

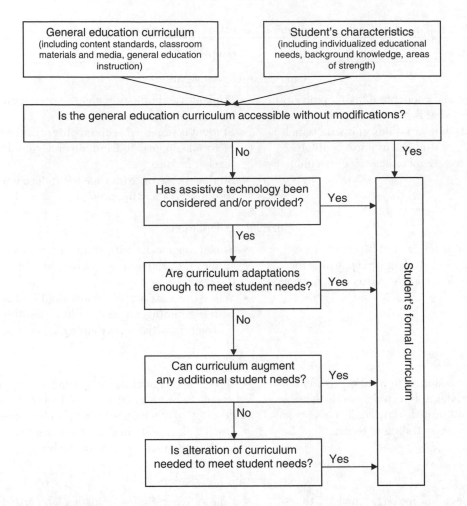

FIGURE 6.1. IEP Team Decision-Making Tool for Curricular Modifications. From Wehmeyer, Lance, and Bashinski (2002). Copyright 2002 by the Council for Exceptional Children. Reprinted by permission.

Diaz-Rico and Weed (2002) outlined a model for developing SDAIE instruction plans that was modified from materials created by the Los Angeles Unified School District (1995)—one of the most linguistically diverse school systems in the United States. This model addressed four components of classroom instruction: content, comprehensibility, connections, and interactions. Content in a SDAIE lessons and curriculum units is planned and organized with general education (e.g., state content standards) and language acquisition outcomes in mind. Diaz-Rico and Weed (p. 121) suggest that teachers should attend to the following three questions in developing language objectives:

1. What is the concept load of the unit and what are the key concepts to demonstrate and illustrate?
2. What are the structures and discourse of the discipline and are these included in the language objectives?

3. Are all four language modes included in planning (listening, speaking, reading, writing)?

Evaluating the appropriateness of curricular materials also is an important content-related aspect of instructional planning. Teachers should make an effort to select materials that provide information in a variety of modalities (e.g., textbooks, video, audio, pictures). In some cases, teachers may need to modify or reorganize materials to make them more accessible to ELLs.

Building connections to students' previous learning and background knowledge is an important aspect of SDAIE lessons. An example of a strategy for building connections is completing know–want–learn (KWL) charts individually and/or as a class (Diaz-Rico & Weed, 2002; see Figure 6.2). Connection building can also be facilitated through the use of semantic mapping and graphic organizers (e.g., Thinking Maps; /www.thinkingmaps.com) and metacognitive strategy instruction (e.g., self-regulated strategy development; Graham & Harris, 2003). To facilitate access, SDAIE instructor must also attend to the comprehensibility of curricular materials. Diaz-Rico and Weed (p. 127) outlined four ways that comprehensibility can be increased:

Topic:

What do I know? (List everything you already know about the topic.)	What do I want to learn? (List things you'd like to learn about the topic.)	What have I learned? (As we study the topic, list what you learned.)

FIGURE 6.2. Template for KWL chart.

1. Contextualization (strategies that create a parallel to speech and/or text through pictures, realia, dramatization, etc.);
2. Modeling (demonstration of the skill or concept to be learned);
3. Speech adjustment (strategies to adjust teacher speech from customary native speech patterns);
4. Comprehension checks (strategies to monitor listening and reading comprehension).

Finally, SDAIE teachers must attend to interaction patterns in their classrooms. In order for students to develop academic understanding and language proficiency, they must have opportunities to converse with peers and present their ideas. Teachers might explore the use of cooperative learning and peer-assisted learning strategies (*kc.vanderbilt.edu/pals*), which have a substantial research base to support their use with diverse populations. Diaz-Rico and Weed (2002) also endorsed the use of representation of information by students as an opportunity to demonstrate understanding. A variety of media and modalities can be employed for re-presentation, including videotaping, student-directed plays, paintings, dioramas, and so forth.

Although SDAIE generally has been associated with instruction for ELLs, teachers of students with disabilities also may apply these strategies. Because many students with disabilities struggle with comprehension and communication, the use of SDAIE strategies may assist teachers in making lessons more accessible.

Thurlow, Albus, Shyyan, Liu, and Barrera (2004) used Multi-Attribute Consensus Building (MACB) with teachers ($n = 30$) of ELLs with disabilities to identify the most widely used and feasible strategies for providing instruction to this population. Table 6.2 presents the instructional strategies that were identify as most used and feasible in reading, mathematics and science. The Thurlow et al. study (see *cehd.umn.edu/nceo/OnlinePubs/ ELLsDisRpt7.pdf*) also includes a number of appendices that educators may find useful when considering possible instructional strategies to support access to the general curriculum for students with disabilities and ELLs.

CONCLUSION

It is our opinion that, although this chapter and the chapter that follows (on universal design for instruction and assessment) appear toward the end of the book, they present concepts and strategies that are essential to implementing inclusive standards-based reform and accountability. Although great progress has been made in developing and validating inclusive assessment techniques, these strategies are of little value unless they are accompanied by classroom-based methods that promote improved performance for students with disabilities and ELLs.

Browder et al. (2007) outlined four reasons why access to the general education curriculum is central to our pursuit of better academic performance and subsequent postschool outcomes for students with disabilities.

TABLE 6.2. Use and Feasibility of Instructional Strategies for ELL Students with Disabilities

Subject	Most used strategies	Most feasible strategies
Reading	1. Teaching pre-, during, and postreading strategies 2. Practicing paraphrasing and retelling strategies 3. Fluency building (high-frequency words) 4. Relating reading to student experiences 5. Direct teaching of vocabulary through listening, seeing, reading and writing in short time segments	1. Relating reading to student experiences 2. Fluency building (high-frequency words) 3. Practicing paraphrasing and retelling strategies 4. Teaching pre-, during, and postreading strategies 5. Graphic organizers such as semantic mapping, story maps, concept maps
Mathematics	1. Adjusted speech 2. Daily relooping of previously learned material 3. Problem solving instruction and task analysis strategies 4. Teacher "think alouds" 5. Ecological approach/ generating data from real-life experiences to use in class	1. Daily relooping of previously learned material 2. Adjusted speech 3. Ecological approach/generating data from real life experiences to use in class 4. Reinforcing math skills through games 5. Tactile, concrete experiences in math
Science	1. Using visuals 2. Teaching how to pick out main idea of text and justify 3. Modeling/teacher demonstration 4. Hands-on, active participation 5. Preteaching vocabulary	1. Using visuals 2. Modeling/teacher demonstration 3. Preteaching vocabulary 4. Hands-on, active participation 5. Using prereading strategies in content areas

Note. From Thurlow, Albus, Shyyan, Liu, and Barrera (2004).

1. The purpose of standards-based reform is to improve adult competence, or (in the words of former Assistant Secretary of Education Diane Ravitch) "standards are created because they improve the 'activity of life'" (1995, p. 9).
2. Although it is unlikely that *all* students with disabilities and ELLs will master the full range of academic skills and concepts at their grade level, many can achieve some degree of academic competence with well-designed, explicit instruction on core skills.
3. Providing access to the general education curriculum is about providing equal educational opportunities to students with disabilities and ELLs.
4. Ensuring access to grade-level curriculum provides students with disabilities and ELLs increased opportunities for self-determination, decision making, and com-

munity involvement. Individuals with limited skills and conceptual understanding are less likely to be fully engaged citizens.

In addition, evaluating access to the general education curriculum is essential for verifying that students with disabilities and ELLs are receiving adequate material resources, appropriate instruction, and ample opportunities to acquire the skills and knowledge they need to be successful. As Scheurich, Skrla, and Johnson (2004) stated, "It is important for us to consider recent history. Before standards and accountability systems, the curriculum provided to low-income students of all races...was typically a 'low-track' one, meaning basic and narrow" (p. 22). The same comment can be applied to the curriculum and instruction that has provided historically for many students with disabilities and ELLs. In an era of standards-based reform and accountability, such a situation is untenable.

7

Universal Design for Instruction and Assessment

Thus far, this book has focused on the need to change aspects of assessment and instruction in order to address the needs of diverse students. The motivation to make these changes stems from recognizing that the way assessment tools and instructional materials typically are designed is not accessible to some students. When assessment and instructional systems are designed to be accessible to the widest variety of students, there is less need for such changes. The notion of designing instructional systems to be accessible to the widest possible group of students has been called *universal design for learning* (UDL; Rose & Meyer, 2006). In this chapter, we discuss the concept of universal design, the legal foundation for applying principles of universal design within educational settings, as well as how this concept can inform instruction and assessment in ways that promote student learning.

As policymakers and IEP teams have struggled to identify what changes are fair *and* maintain the integrity of tests for the diverse students with whom they work, they are often forced to examine whether such changes would be similarly helpful to students who do not have the unique characteristics of the target students. In many cases, it can be difficult to argue that various accommodations are differentially effective for students with disabilities. For instance, many students—including those without disabilities—may have reading difficulties. When tests are designed with the assumption that all students taking the tests will be proficient readers, it may be difficult for many students (e.g., students with lower-than-proficient reading skills) to demonstrate their knowledge on the tests. In such cases, it may seem unfair to make changes only for those with disabilities, when the change may actually allow for better assessment and instruction of targeted skills for many other students. Similarly, when instructional materials are developed that assume students are able to read at a particular reading level, it may limit access to learning not only among those with reading disabilities, but also among those who have general reading difficulties that are not associated with a particular disability. By carefully considering the goals for assessment and instruction from the very beginning, along with the various challenges that diverse students may encounter in their attempts to demonstrate their knowledge, those who develop assessment and instructional materials can potentially improve testing and learning for all students.

Dolan (2000) suggested that learning goals need to be very carefully articulated prior to developing a system to measure whether students have met those goals. By carefully considering whether reading comprehension (as opposed to comprehension of oral language) is something that relates to the learning goal of a particular unit, lesson, or standard, one can then determine whether instruction and assessment materials need to be presented in a written format or whether they can potentially be presented in different ways. By carefully considering the ultimate learning goals, those who design assessment and instructional materials can be proactive in making sure that the materials accurately address the given learning goals for all students. Through application of the principles of universal design, these considerations can be addressed, leading to instructional and assessment systems that are fair and highly accessible to all students.

THE CONCEPT OF UNIVERSAL DESIGN

Universal design is a concept that was first articulated within the field of architecture. Typically, structures have been designed and built to be accessible to individuals who have the ability to walk, who currently make up the majority of humanity. However, various features of building interiors and exteriors, such as ramps and curb cuts, have been associated with creating greater access to buildings among individuals who cannot walk. What is particularly exciting about these design features is that they have made a positive difference in the lives of a variety of individuals in addition to those who have a permanent inability to walk. For instance, those who are temporarily injured or those who carry heavy loads of materials using rolling carts find ramps and curb cuts particularly helpful. Another example includes the application of closed captioning on television for the deaf and hard of hearing. Although this feature was intended to make television accessible to a particular group of individuals, a variety of different individuals benefit from this feature, including those who may want to watch television while others in the room want to be engaged in a different activity. By considering people with "special" needs in the design phases of building structures, a product that is better for everyone often emerges.

Through application of the principles of universal design, it is anticipated that structures and systems can be developed that are much more accessible and less stigmatizing for individuals with unique needs. As technology advances and people with serious injuries and severe disabilities are able to receive the medical treatment that they need to live longer and more productive lives, accessibility is something that can be of great benefit not only to the associated individuals, but also society more generally. By not paying attention to the needs of such individuals, these incredibly valuable contributions to society may be lost. Often, through just minor changes in how material is presented or designed, many more individuals can access and learn from it. Very frequently, this has the added benefit of being much more user friendly to society in general.

LEGAL REQUIREMENTS FOR UNIVERSAL DESIGN IN EDUCATION

Universal design was first mentioned in educationally related law in the Assistive Technology Act of 1998. The focus of this law was to promote consideration of universal design principles in the development and use of various technologies that could benefit people with disabilities across a variety of environments. Later, rules and regulations developed to address IDEA 2004 indicated that some state funds were intended to be used "to support the use of technology, including technology with universal design principles and assistive technology devices, to maximize accessibility to the general education curriculum for children with disabilities." IDEA 2004 further mentioned the National Instructional Materials Accessibility Standard (NIMAS), which is intended to support educational agencies in the development of accessible instructional materials. The regulations further require that state and districtwide educational assessments be developed according to *universal design* principles. These federal requirements indicate that the concept of universal design is something that all must become familiar with and should be evident across all learning and assessment environments.

PRINCIPLES OF UNIVERSAL DESIGN

The Center for Universal Design at North Carolina State University describes seven principles of universal design (Center for Universal Design, 1997). These include the following:

Equitable use. The design is useful and marketable to people with diverse abilities.

Flexibility in use. The design accommodates a wide range of individual preferences and abilities.

Simple and intuitive. Use of the design is easy to understand, regardless of the user's experience, knowledge, language skills, or current concentration level.

Perceptible information. The design communicates necessary information effectively to the user, regardless of ambient conditions or the user's sensory abilities.

Tolerance for error. The design minimizes hazards and the adverse consequences of accidental or unintended actions.

Low physical effort. The design can be used efficiently and comfortably and with a minimum of fatigue.

Size and space for approach and use. Appropriate size and space is provided for approach, reach, manipulation, and use regardless of user's body size, posture, or mobility. Copyright © 1997 NC State University, The Center for Universal Design.

UNIVERSAL DESIGN FOR LEARNING

Over the past few years, the Center for Applied Special Technology (CAST) has been developing a framework for UDL. David Rose, director of CAST, has articulated how individuals vary in terms of the recognition, strategic, and affective networks that they draw on to learn new information and skills (Rose, 2001). Because of these individual differences, it is important to provide as much flexibility as possible to support students in attaining a set of learning goals, once those goals have been carefully determined. According to the CAST website (*www.cast.org*), UDL involves providing:

- *Multiple means of representation*, to give learners various ways of acquiring information and knowledge.
- *Multiple means of expression*, to provide learners alternatives for demonstrating what they know.
- *Multiple means of engagement*, to tap unto learners' interests, offer appropriate challenges, and increase motivation.

When teachers consider each of these strategies in designing their lessons, their instruction may become much more accessible to all students. The CAST website provides a variety of examples and tools that can guide teachers in applying the principles of UDL to their classrooms. A checklist for exploring applications of the principles of UDL to instruction is provided in Appendix 7.1. Additional ideas for promoting UDL are provided in Hitchcock et al. (2002).

Innovations in technology are making it possible to present material in a variety of different ways and can allow students to choose the method of presentation that best suits their needs. Computer programs that allow students to have a computer read material to them that is available in electronic formats have been developed. Similarly, software that can translate written material into different languages is available. Podcasts are becoming a more widely used way of communicating information. Furthermore, digital recorders and computer recording programs can allow students to record oral responses, rather than having to demonstrate their knowledge and skill primarily in written format. Hyperlinks can allow students to quickly learn the meanings of unfamiliar words that are used in electronic texts, making it possible for students with limited vocabulary to build their vocabulary and understand what they are reading in an efficient manner. When teachers make use of these technologies in instruction, it benefits not only students who might struggle when required to obtain and demonstrate knowledge through reading and writing, but also all those who will likely need to make use of these new technologies to be successful in quickly obtaining and using material in the information age.

Furthermore, packaged educational materials are beginning to be developed from the beginning using the concepts of universal design. For example, the Thinking Reader® (Tom Snyder Productions, Scholastic), which was designed by David Rose and Bridget Dalton of CAST, is a product that provides multiple ways for students to access a variety of novels commonly used in middle-school English courses. The package includes paper versions of the novels, as well as computerized versions in which the teacher can determine the level of scaffolding needed for a student to comprehend the novel (e.g., the program can be set to require students to engage in various comprehension strategies such as audio-recording a short summary of each page before moving on, and if the student can't come up with a summary, to hear one read, etc.). Tools like this can make it possible for all students to have access to the same content, no matter what their current reading and writing skill level happens to be.

Readers are encouraged to examine the "Teaching Every Student" section of the CAST website (*www.cast.org/teachingeverystudent*) for additional support in applying the principles of UDL in their classrooms. It is anticipated that the role of the teacher will not be diminished but will instead evolve, as do other occupations, with application of UDL technology (Pisha & Coyne, 2001).

UNIVERSAL DESIGN FOR ASSESSMENT

Just as UDL is making better instruction and learning possible for all students, application of the principles of universal design to large-scale assessment systems has the potential to allow for better assessment of all students. The National Center on Educational Outcomes has created the "Universal Design Online Manual" to guide states in the development of tests that can be considered to adhere to the principles of universal design. Johnstone, Altman, and Thurlow (2006) suggest that the following considerations be made when designing assessments to be accessible to a wide variety of students (we have elaborated on these considerations to convey their meaning).

- *Intended constructs are measured.* Often, the tools that are used for assessing student knowledge and skill require that students have certain prerequisite skills (e.g., reading and writing skills), such that without these skills, the intended constructs of the test (e.g., social studies knowledge, science knowledge) may not be adequately measured.
- *Respect for the diversity of the assessment population.* Items need to be selected such that varying levels of prior knowledge (across examinees) related to the content of the item are reduced. For example, an item related to blizzards may not be understood by those living in a part of the country, or recently moving from a part of the country, that does not encounter blizzards.
- *Concise and readable text.* It is important to eliminate, as much as possible, extra words or complicated ways of presenting written material.
- *Clear format for test.* Introducing a complicated format may cause those who are not savvy in test taking to perform lower simply due to poorly developed test-taking skills rather than due to actual differences in the skills intended to be measured.
- *Clear visuals.* Although it may seem more engaging and stimulating to add a lot of detail to the visuals presented on tests, this can distract some students and cause difficulty for students in obtaining the information needed from the visual to demonstrate their knowledge and skill.
- *Changes allowed to format without changing meaning or difficulty.* Usually, allowing multiple formats for skill and knowledge demonstration is advantageous. However, in some cases, this may actually make the test easier with respect to what is intended to be measured. For example, if a test is intended to measure written language skills, then an oral responses may change the meaning and difficulty level of the test.

A checklist for thinking about how to apply the principles of universal design in assessment is provided in Appendix 7.2. Thompson, Johnstone, and Thurlow (2002) and Johnstone, Thompson, Moen, Bolt, and Kato (2005) describe various methods that might be used to examine item-level performance in order to identify any potential problems with items for various student subgroups. Application of these methods may help ensure that items are appropriate for a wide variety of students.

Just as with UDL, universal design for assessment can be promoted through advancing the application of computer technology in schools. Computerized test administrations are becoming much more common and can allow students to control elements such as font style and size, presentation modes (auditory and written), and response modes (oral and written). Dolan, Hall, Banerjee, Chun, and Strangman (2005) conducted a study to examine the potential benefits of a computer-based test that had a screen-reader option, and students scored significantly higher on that condition than on a paper-and-pencil test when items included reading passages that were more than 100 words in length. However, in places where students have limited access to computers, they may not be prepared to take computerized tests. It is important for the design of assessments to match, as much as possible, how instruction is provided in the classroom. As students begin to use computers more frequently in instruction, it is likely that they will be prepared and feel comfortable in using a computer when taking tests. Because computers can facilitate multiple modes of presentation and response, computerized test administration is considered to be highly advantageous for districts and states to pursue now and in the future.

EXAMPLE: UNIVERSAL DESIGN FOR LEARNING

The following represents how instruction in a state standard might be addressed in a traditional format, as well as in a way that incorporates many more principles of UDL.

- *State standard.* "The student will read and demonstrate comprehension of nonfiction; the student will use text organizers, such as type, headings, and graphics, to predict and categorize information" (modified Virginia English Standard 5. 6[a]).
- *Summary of lesson that shows limited application of the principles of universal design.* The teacher reads aloud from an informational text for the class. The teacher points to and reads the headings in her book prior to reading the text and asks students to think about what they already know about the heading topics. She also points to the diagrams included in the text and explains what they are showing related to the text. She explains that words in bold type are key vocabulary words, and that the definitions of these words can be found in the glossary. She demonstrates use of the glossary with an example word. After she has finished reading the informational text, she provides students with a worksheet (see Figure 7.1) that they are asked to complete individually, using an upcoming chapter from their social studies textbook.

Using this approach, students are provided the instruction orally, and have the opportunity to learn about the concepts if they can see the headings and diagrams presented by the teacher at the beginning of the class session. Independent practice requires that the

Student name: _____

1. List the headings of the text below:

2. What do you already know about that relates to these headings?

3. How many diagrams are there in this text? Provide a brief illustration of one of the diagrams below and explain what it shows in your own words.

4. Identify two words that you did not know the meaning of that were bolded keywords in this text. Provide the definitions below.

    a. Word: _____. Definition:

    b. Word: _____ Definition:

FIGURE 7.1. Example of worksheet used for instruction.

students know how to read and write, and that they are interested in the social studies material presented.

- *Lesson that shows greater application of the principles of universal design.* In order to improve presentation and make it accessible to more students, the teacher might consider using various visual aids to allow more students to view the headings and diagrams that she initially describes, along with providing the information verbally. A document camera might be used to magnify the text features (i.e., headings, diagrams, glossary, etc.) that the teacher is intending to teach students how to use within informational texts. The teacher might consider having students work in small groups, with each student assigned to report to the small group on one of the aspects included on the worksheet above. Groups could be assigned to include students of a variety of skill levels, and perhaps selected to work together based on a common interest in a given area. The selected text could be different for each group and could be an informational text related to their common interest, and available in paper format and electronic format (either on the Internet or scanned in to the computer, to allow for changing font or having the text read aloud for those students with reading difficulties). The teacher could assign each student in a group to a different text feature (i.e., identify all headings, identify two bolded vocabulary words that at least two members of the group do not know, explain a diagram, etc.), with easier tasks assigned to those of lower skill levels and more difficult tasks assigned to more advanced students. Although individual students would be primarily responsible for their given task, they would then be required to share their findings with the small group, and ask for feedback from the small group on whether they adequately addressed the given text feature. The small group could then report back to the entire class how they learned about each text feature with their given book. Each individual's task could be reported on through a written summary, an oral explanation, or a drawing/diagram (multiple forms of expression) presented to the class.

EXAMPLE: UNIVERSAL DESIGN FOR ASSESSMENT

- *State standard*: "The student will analyze problem situations, including games of chance, board games, or grading scales, and make predictions, using knowledge of probability" (Virginia Math Standard 8.11).
- *Test item that shows limited application of the principles of universal design.*

> Suppose you are playing blackjack with five friends using a 52-card deck of playing cards. You and your friends are having a great time, and have already played five rounds of this. You have won three of the rounds. In the sixth round, you are the first to be dealt a card. Your five friends are then dealt a card, and then you are dealt a second card. What is the chance that you are initially dealt the jack of spades, and then are dealt a card that is of the suit of diamonds?

This item requires that students have substantial prior knowledge of a deck of playing cards. It also includes quite a bit of background and contextual information that is not needed to answer the item correctly (e.g., friends are having a great time, you have already played five rounds, etc.). Someone who has difficulty reading may get lost in reading this extra information, which may hinder his or her ability to demonstrate underlying math skills and knowledge related to what the item is intended to measure.

- *Test item that shows greater application of the principles of universal design.*

> What is the chance that if you spin this spinner two times, it will land on a section with a smile (☺) and then land on a section with a diamond (♦)? (*Assume all sections have equal area.*)

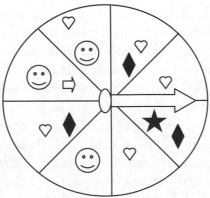

The following description of this figure could also be provided. "The spinner has an equal chance of landing on eight different sections. Five sections contain hearts, three sections contain diamonds, three sections have smiles, one has a star, and one has an arrow."

- *Technology applications.* Advancing technology can make it possible for students to adapt test items to meet their unique needs. For instance, items that contain a lot of written text, but are not intended to measure decoding skills, can be presented on computers and students can then access screen readers to have the items read aloud as they deem necessary based on their own personal desires. Furthermore, electronic test formats can allow students to enlarge items that they find difficult to read because of visual impairments. Computerized tests also can include video clips to make certain items more "real-to-life," and engage students in using the particular skill on which they are being tested. In some cases, students may be able to respond orally within a computer administration and have their answers recorded for later scoring, rather than being required to write their responses. Furthermore, computer adaptive tests have been developed to ensure accurate measurement at each possible level of mastery and engage students in testing at their current level of functioning. Although security issues may prevent the use of electronic tests for some purposes, as test security strategies advance, it is likely that computerized testing will become more common and may allow students better access to demonstrating their skills and knowledge with respect to what is intended to be measured.

APPENDIX 7.1

Universal Design for Learning: Checking Accessibility

1. What is the learning goal(s) for this lesson?

2. What plans do I have for *presenting* the material?

    - Textbook/reading materials
    - Textbook/reading materials to address the needs of students at a variety of reading levels
    - Electronic texts to allow students to enlarge print as necessary (can be scanned in)
    - Electronic texts (can be scanned in), as well as screen readers to allow students who need the material read aloud to have that available
    - Oral presentation of material by teacher
    - Written presentation of material by teacher
    - Video clips demonstrating key concepts (with closed captioning)
    - Podcasts of orally presented material are available
    - Links to pertinent websites for students to explore

3. What plans do I have for how students can *express* their learning?

    - Written assignment
    - Students can use word processor, spell checkers, calculators, thesaurus
    - Study guides that highlight main concepts – students need to fill in
    - Multiple study guides that may provide different levels of support depending on initial student knowledge/skill – students need to fill in
    - Illustrations
    - Oral recording for assignment
    - Video recording
    - Individual project
    - Structured group project
    - Group project with individual accountability "built-in"
    - Group discussion
    - Class discussion

4. What plans do I have for how students might become *engaged* in learning?

    - Do students have choice for topics to explore?
    - Do students have choice for ways to express their learning?
    - Do students have ways for monitoring their own progress toward goals?
    - Do students have choice/input in how they are rewarded?
    - Are there multiple levels of challenge to ensure that each student is challenged, but does not become overly frustrated?
    - Has the goal for learning been explicitly connected to real-world applications?

Universal Design for Assessment: Checking Accessibility

1. What standards are intended to be assessed?

2. Do the selected items require prior knowledge and skill that are not intended to be assessed? (*If you answer yes, revise assessment to eliminate these aspects of items.*)

3. If the assessment is presented in written format, is the text concise and easily understood? In the case of a test intended to measure reading skills, is the text of the appropriate difficulty level?

4. Are students familiar with the assessment format? Will it be relatively easy for them to follow the directions in completing test items?

5. If there are any visuals in the test, are they clear? If the test is not intended to measure a student's ability to gain knowledge from the visuals, can the information be presented in a different format to ensure those with visual impairments can demonstrate knowledge and skill?

6. Is the test amenable to alternative formats (i.e., can be presented electronically to facilitate various accommodations such as screen reader, larger font, etc.)?

7. Is the grading/scoring rubric consistent with measuring only those standards intended to be assessed?

8

Conclusion

The introduction and implementation of federal policies like NCLB and the reauthorized IDEA have resulted in increased scrutiny for and pressure on educators, including those who work with students with disabilities and ELLs. The U.S. education system has entered an era of stringent accountability where programs and practices must demonstrate their effectiveness in improving student outcomes. This push for more accountability reflects recent trends advocating results-oriented government and performance-based budgeting (Harbin, Rous, & McLean, 2005). In 1993, Congress codified the importance of measuring outcomes when they enacted the Government Performance and Results Act (GPRA). As a result of GPRA, the U.S. Department of Education and other federal agencies are required to clearly define goals and desired outcomes for funded programs, develop specific indicators to measure these goals, and report the data on an annual basis (Roach, McGrath, & Wixson, 2008). Thus, although inclusive standards-based reform and accountability systems may feel uniquely punitive to educators and other stakeholders, these policies only reflect a larger move toward results-oriented policymaking.

When educators consider the larger policy contexts surrounding inclusive standards-based reform and accountability, it should be apparent that academic standards, large-scale assessments, and public reporting of school performance are unlikely to disappear in the near future. Instead of hoping for a dramatic shift in educational policy, we hope educators and other stakeholders will use the information in this book to take a proactive stance toward inclusive standards-based reform and accountability. To assist readers in advocating for best practice in their classrooms and schools, this chapter provides an overview of professional standards for assessments and accountability that have developed by various organizations. In addition, we conclude with some "talking points" on the importance and value of inclusive standards-based reform and accountability. We hope that these "big ideas" will assist readers in their discussions and consultations with other educators and family members regarding the inclusion of students with disabilities and ELLs in the general education curriculum and large-scale assessments.

STANDARDS FOR THE DESIGN AND USE OF INCLUSIVE ASSESSMENT AND ACCOUNTABILITY SYSTEMS

In order to ensure that inclusive assessment and accountability systems meet certain thresholds for technical documentation and appropriate implementation, various organizations have created standards documents. Of these, the most prominent is the *Standards for Educational and Psychological Testing* (1999) which is a joint publication of the American Educational Research Association, the American Psychological Association, and the National Council on Measurement in Education. This is an extensive document that addresses a variety of issues applicable to inclusive assessment and accountability. The *Standards* are intended "to provide criteria for the evaluation of tests, testing practices, and the effects of test use.... The *Standards* provide a frame of reference to assure that relevant issues are addressed" in developing and interpreting tests (p. 2). Although it is beyond the scope of this book to outline all 15 chapters of the *Standards*, we believe it is essential that all educators and policymakers involved in assessment and accountability systems become familiar with its contents. As we are preparing this book, a new (seventh) edition of the *Standards* is being finalized.

Standards for Teacher Competence in Educational Assessment of Students

The American Federation of Teachers in conjunction with the National Council on Measurement in Education and the National Education Association published the *Standards for Teacher Competence in Educational Assessment of Students* (American Federation of Teachers, National Council on Measurement in Education & National Education Association, 1990). This document outlined a variety of assessment-related skills and concepts considered essential to support effective teaching practices. Moreover, according to the document, the standards were intended to serve as impetus for "teachers to demonstrate skill at selecting, developing, applying, using, communicating, and evaluating student assessment information and student assessment practices" (¶10).

According to this set of standards, teachers should be skilled in:

1. Choosing assessment methods appropriate for instructional decisions;
2. Developing assessment methods appropriate for instructional decisions;
3. Administering, scoring and interpreting the results of both externally-produced and teacher-produced assessment methods;
4. Using assessment results when making decisions about individual students, planning teaching, developing curriculum, and school improvement;
5. Developing valid pupil grading procedures which use pupil assessments.
6. Communicating assessment results to students, parents, other lay audiences, and other educators; and
7. Recognizing unethical, illegal, and otherwise inappropriate assessment methods and uses of assessment information.

Although these standards have broad application in regards to teachers' use of many different forms of assessment, they also have specific applicability to inclusive assessment and accountability systems. For example, these standards call on educators to administer, score, and interpret large-scale assessments and alternate assessments in a competent and ethical manner. According to these standards, teachers also should develop skill in communicating and interpreting the results of tests used in the accountability system for a variety of stakeholders. Certainly, attention to these standards in teacher preparation programs and inservice professional development would make teachers more informed test users and consumers. Additional information on these standards is available on through the Buros Institute on Mental Measurements: *www.unl.edu/buros/bimm/html/article3.html*.

Principles and Characteristics of Inclusive Assessment and Accountability Systems

The National Center for Educational Outcomes (NCEO) has developed a framework of six core principles for the design and implementation of inclusive assessment and accountability systems (see Appendix 8.1). These core principles are intended to go beyond compliance with federal policy (e.g., NCLB, IDEA) to reflect areas and opportunities where research and practice suggest there can be important benefits to students, their families, and educators. The core principles are based on the NCEO staff's ongoing, extensive experiences providing technical assistance and consultation to state departments of education, school districts, and individual educators. In addition, the principles were subject to review and comment from multiple stakeholder groups, including teachers and school administrators; parents of students with disabilities; state department assessment, general education, and special education staff; state and federal policymakers; and regional and national leaders in educational assessment and accountability (Thurlow, Quenemoen, Thompson, & Lehr, 2001).

Much like current federal policy, NCEO Principle 1 embraces the goal that *all* students will be included in state- and district-level assessment systems. As discussed in previous chapters of this book, most students with disabilities and ELLs will complete the same large-scale assessment(s) administered to the general population of students with or without testing accommodations. For a small number of students with disabilities and ELLs, an alternate assessment may be appropriate. In order to achieve 100% participation, it is important that educators *never* exempt or exclude students from the accountability system solely because of their disability or English language proficiency (Thurlow et al., 2001).

NCEO Principle 2 addresses how educators make decisions regarding student participation in the accountability systems. In particular, it is essential that participation decisions "are based on the student's ability to show what she or he knows and is able to do in the assessment formats available to all students—not on the student's instructional program, current level of functioning, or expectations about how well a student will perform" (Thurlow et al., 2001, p. 7). To this end, IEP teams need to have knowledge of allowable testing accommodations and available alternate forms of assessment. IEP teams also need to document their decision-making process regarding participation, including consideration of students' present level of performance, involvement in the general education curriculum, and typical accommodations (i.e., supports and scaffolds) provided during classroom instruction. Chapter 2 of this book provides information to support educators' participation decisions.

NCEO Principles 3 and 4 concern the reporting of scores from state and district accountability systems. Again, it is important that *all* students are included in this component of standards-based assessment and accountability. Moreover, reflecting NCLB regulations, school districts and states must provide aggregated and disaggregated reporting of student performance, so that stakeholders can identify where to focus instructional improvement efforts. Particular attention must be given to the comprehensibility of reports provided to different stakeholder groups. Assessment scores and results that can not be understood and interpreted by educators, family members, and policymakers are likely to be viewed as inconsequential for guiding practice and policy. Moreover, NCEO's recommendations indicate the performance of different student subgroups must count equally in any index of school and district performance (e.g., the reporting of AYP). Early state responses to NCLB illustrated that this approach was either not understood or ignored by state-level policymakers. Many states chose to establish larger cell sizes for AYP reporting for some student subgroups (e.g., 40 students for students with disabilities and ELL vs. 30 students for all other subgroups). This decision effectively limited consideration of these subgroups' achievement when evaluating AYP at the school and (in some cases) the district level.

Monitoring performance over time and providing professional development to educators to support improved outcomes is the focus of NCEO Principle 5. Clearly, monitoring changes in participation rates and student performance is one of the central outcomes of accountability systems. The administration of large-scale assessments and alternate assessments has resulted in an increased amount of information regarding educational systems' performance. Creation of this wealth of data, however, is unlikely to produce improvement without appropriate interpretation and action from educators and policymakers. To support appropriate understanding of and responses to assessment information, training to promote assessment literacy is necessary for each of these groups. This training is especially important to support the participation and progress of students with disabilities and ELL students. For these subgroups, participation decisions (and in some cases alternate assessment strategies) are dependent on the understanding and professional judgment of educators.

NCEO Principle 6 reaffirms the assumption that *all* students should be included in assessment and accountability systems. In particular, this assumption should guide educators' practice decisions and educational leaders' policymaking. By affirming and striving to enact these principles, educators can "enhance the positive consequences and reduce the negative consequences . . . of assessment and accountability systems . . . and (move) toward systems that are designed to be more inclusive" (Thurlow et al., 2001, p. 4). To support this work, NCEO has developed a set of checklists based on the *Principles*. These evaluative tools are available as part of *The Self Study Guide to Inclusive Assessment and Accountability Systems* (Quenemoen, Thompson, Thurlow, & Lehr, 2001; *cehd.umn.edu/NCEO/ OnlinePubs/workbook.pdf*).

FEA Principles and Recommendations for Federal Law and State and Local Systems

In June 2007, the Forum on Educational Accountability (FEA) convened an Expert Panel on Assessment, consisting of leaders in the field of educational testing, to prepare a report outlining guiding principles and recommendations for policymakers and educational leaders in revising NCLB. The assessment experts who drafted the report, *Assessment and Accountability for Improving Schools and Learning*, indicated that significant revisions were necessary for NCLB to facilitate educational equity and improved outcomes for all students. The panel created a set of recommendations built around six guiding principles, providing a framework for the creation of "an inclusive, beneficial, and fair assessment and accountability system within a strong, equitable, and steadily improving educational system" (Forum on Educational Accountability, 2007). The full text of these principles and recommendations are provided in Appendix 8.2.

In FEA Principle I, the panel members identified efforts to insure that all students have equal access and opportunities to learn as essential for improving NCLB. To meet this goal, additional resources are needed to support equity in material resources and personnel preparation across schools and communities. In addition, the panel members advocated a movement away from "one-size-fits-all" programming in response to NCLB regulations, preferring that schools and districts implement policies and regulations in ways that made sense for their contexts.

FEA Principle II addresses the creation of comprehensive state and local assessment systems. To meet this objective, states and districts need to collaborate to create a seamless set of assessments (classroom-based and standardized) that can guide instructional planning and monitor student progress. For example, states and districts might invest resources to implement the Dynamic Indicators of Basic Early Literacy Skills (DIBELS; *dibels.uoregon. edu*), a series of brief curriculum-based measurement probes that are highly predictive of student performance on large-scale, end-of-year assessments. DIBELS measures are time- and resource-efficient assessments of key skills in early reading providing data that can (1) guide teachers' instructional planning and (2) facilitate identification of students who may need additional intervention support to achieve proficiency on achievement tests.

Developing and implementing inclusive assessment strategies is the focus of FEA Principle III. The panel members endorsed the importance of many of the ideas and tactics discussed in previous chapters of this book including testing accommodations, alternate assessments, and universal design. In addition, the panel called for ongoing federal support of research to develop and validate inclusive assessment strategies. Along these lines, FEA Principle IV calls for reconceptualization of accountability reporting under NCLB. Currently, federal regulations use a status model where students' performance is considered "proficient" when they achieve a certain score on the state large-scale assessment. These status models do not index individual students' progress in acquiring skills and concepts measured by the state tests. For example, a student with a relatively low score (e.g., 10% of items correct) on a large-scale assessment could make substantial growth but still not achieve the cut score (e.g., 60% of items correct) for "proficient" performance on the test. Moreover, in the status model currently employed under NCLB, a student getting 10% of the items correct and another student who got 50% correct are considered "not yet proficient" for AYP reporting. In this case, the performance of these two students is considered indistinguishable, and no credit is conferred on schools and school districts that support student progress unless those students move from "not yet proficient" to "proficient" as measured by state tests. The panel members suggested that regulations be changed to support descriptions of "school performance in terms of status, improvement, and growth, using the states' multiple sources of evidence" rather than relying only on the results of large-scale assessments (p. 7).

FEA Principle V encourages states and school districts to continue to conduct research to validate their accountability systems. To that end, the panel members endorsed NCLB's disaggregation of performance by student subgroups. However, the panel felt that information on student achievement in additional subject areas (beyond reading/language arts, mathematics, and science) might be successfully integrated into inclusive accountability and assessment systems. Another area for additional research and advocacy is the identification of rigorous, but realistic targets for performance because NCLB's current expectation (i.e., 100% of students "proficient" by 2013–2014), though attractive in its clarity, is unlikely to be attainable in practice. Finally, the panel members focused FEA Principle VI on the application of assessment information to guide school improvement efforts. Because resources in most systems are relatively scarce, it is important that additional research be conducted to determine that AYP decisions correctly identify which schools (or classrooms) are in need of additional support.

WHY INCLUSIVE ACCOUNTABILITY AND CURRICULAR ACCESS ARE IMPORTANT

Read the following scenario[1] and imagine how you might feel if you were a teacher at this school. How would you feel if you were one of the students? How would you feel if you were a student with a disability? How would you feel if you were the parent of a student with a disability?

Next Friday is "School Picture Day" at Sunnyside Elementary. Mrs. Flanagan, the principal, has made arrangements for Truscott Photography to take individual and class pictures. Information packets have been sent home to students' families regarding Picture Day and the cost of purchasing various photo packages. The Parent-Teacher Association has agreed to have parents on hand throughout the day to help collect payments and order forms from the students as they come to the cafeteria to have their pictures taken.

Mrs. Flanagan feels relatively certain everything will run smoothly on Picture Day, but she has some concerns about the involvement of the students in the school's program for autism and pervasive developmental disabilities. She feels like their behavior can be unpredictable and worries that the stress and excitement of Picture Day might

[1]Thank you to Steve Elliott for sharing a version of this scenario with us.

upset them or make them anxious. Mrs. Flanagan decides to talk to Mr. Hernandez, the special education teacher who works with this group of students, to see if they can arrange a field trip for the class on Picture Day. She feels like a trip to the park would be an appropriate and less stressful alternate activity for these students.

How would you react if you were Mr. Hernandez? Most of us probably would feel shocked that Mrs. Flanagan would suggest that students with disabilities should not participate in Picture Day. We might be concerned that these students' parents would be upset that they are being excluded. We might question whether the other students in the classrooms that include the students with autism will wonder why their classmates are not in the class picture. No doubt, you believe that Mrs. Flanagan's decision making is, at best, misguided and probably could be described as unfair and discriminatory. Although not a perfectly analogous situation, until recently decision making and policy surrounding the inclusion of students with disabilities and ELLs in standards-based reform and accountability systems often was equally misguided, unfair, and (possibly) discriminatory.

WHAT'S MEASURED IS WHAT MATTERS

One of the purposes of accountability systems is to provide an accounting (or picture) of what students are learning. When students with disabilities and ELLs are excluded from the accountability "picture," it is impossible for educators, families, and other stakeholders to get an accurate sense of how students, schools, and districts are performing (Elliott, Braden, & White, 2001). Perhaps you have heard someone say "what's measured is what matters." In many cases, this statement can be applied to the participation in assessment and accountability systems by students with disabilities and ELLs. When these students are excluded from accountability systems, it reinforces the message that their performance does not really matter. Early in his career as an elementary schoolteacher, the second author overheard an administrator make the following comment to a fellow teacher: "I don't care what you do with those students with disabilities as long as you keep them in your classroom." For too long, this sort of thinking was all too typical of the sentiments of many general educators and school administrators. Inclusive standards-based reform and accountability, however, has changed the attitudes and actions of many educators.

INCLUSIVE STANDARDS-BASED REFORM
AND ACCOUNTABILITY SUPPORT CURRICULAR ACCESS

When *every* student is included, educators and policymakers have increased motivation to insure that each student receives access to and opportunities to learn the skills and concepts on state and district large-scale assessments. For example, accountability has resulted in increased research on teaching mathematics and science concepts to diverse groups of students. In fact, over the previous few years, multiple federal grants have been awarded to research instructional and curricular innovations in these areas. This research is important to developing and disseminating more effective methods to support the academic learning of diverse groups of students, particularly students with cognitive disabilities like autism and mental retardation.

In his book *New Directions in Special Education: Eliminating Ableism in Policy and Practice*, former U.S. Department of Education Office of Special Education Programs director Thomas Hehir (2005) uses the concept of *ableism* as a frame for examining the educational supports and services provided to students with disabilities. Ableism is discrimination and oppression based on the assumption that people with disabilities have fewer abilities and, therefore, less value to society. Hehir writes:

> Applied to schooling and child development, ableist prejudices become particularly apparent. The devaluation of disability results in societal attitudes that uncritically assert that it is better for a child to walk than roll, speak than sign, read print than read Braille, spell independently than use a spell-check.... In short, in the eyes of many educators and society, it is preferable for disabled students to do things the same way as their non-disabled peers. (p. 16)

It is important that educators avoid ableist assumptions in the development and implementation of standards-based reform and accountability systems. Although federal policy requires access to and progress in the general education curriculum, it does not require that *all* students participate in instruction and demonstrate their achievement in the same manner. This same conceptual frame can be extended to ELL students as well; when students are working to acquire English proficiency, educators have a responsibility to consider a variety of instructional modalities for providing curricular access and opportunity to learn.

INCLUSIVE STANDARDS-BASED REFORM AND ACCOUNTABILITY *CAN* PRODUCE POSITIVE OUTCOMES

One interesting outcome of the implementation of standards-based alternate assessments is the growing amount of anecdotal evidence of its effects on students' access to and progress in the general education curriculum. Many teachers have expressed surprise and excitement at the scope of academic skills and concepts students with significant cognitive disabilities are able to master. In a presentation at the Office of Special Education Programs Project Directors' meeting, Warlick and Towles-Reeves (2005) shared the following comments regarding influence of inclusive accountability on the educational experiences of students with significant disabilities:

> *Teacher:* I used to pride myself on being a good caregiver. Alternate assessment taught me to be a good teacher.
>
> *Parent:* I first thought testing these kids was crazy. All I wanted was for the school to keep my child safe, warm, and nourished. Thanks to alternate assessment, we learned my child could learn, can communicate, and make choices.

We have heard many similar comments in our work to support educators in implementing inclusive standards-based reform and accountability systems. Anecdotal evidence like this is encouraging and suggests that these policies may be producing meaningful changes in the educational experiences of students with disabilities and ELLs. To build on these comments, teachers, administrators, and educational researchers must collaborate to collect data evidence and conduct systematic evaluations of the impact of standards-based reform and accountability. "Research is needed on the overall impact of the new emphasis on academic achievement for (these groups) . . . and on the impact of academic instruction on the transition to adult living. . . . Research is needed on how parents value the types of skills being taught . . . and how students respond to these opportunities" (Browder et al., 2007, p. 14). Additional investigations on the impact of inclusive standards-based reform and accountability systems on outcomes for diverse populations will assist educators and other stakeholders in determining "what works" in these policies and what components need to be improved or replaced.

EQUITY AND OPPORTUNITY ARE CENTRAL TO INCLUSIVE STANDARDS-BASED REFORM AND ACCOUNTABILITY

Central to inclusive standards-based reform and accountability is the belief that setting clear and rigorous academic standards, requiring teaching and learning in schools to focus on these standards, and measuring and reporting students' academic progress via large-scale assessments can serve as an impetus for improved educational quality across states and school districts. Early supporters of standards-based reform viewed it as a powerful tool to increase students' opportunities to learn and promote equity across classrooms, schools, and communities (Resnick, Rothman, Slattery, & Vranek, 2003; Roach & Elliott, in press). Scheurlich et al. (2004) stated, "No matter what each of us values most as a pathway to equity, educational accountability has become the primary public space in which most of the discussion about . . . inequities in public education is now occurring" (p. 15). As such, educators who work with students with disabilities and ELLs cannot afford to be disengaged from or disinterested in development and implementation of inclusive standards-based reform and accountability systems (Roach & Elliott). To that end, we hope that the information in this book will support educators in facilitating improved access and outcomes for the diverse student populations in their classrooms and schools.

Principles and Characteristics of Inclusive Assessment and Accountability Systems

Principle I. All students with disabilities are included in the assessment system.

Characteristic 1.1. All students in all settings who receive educational services are included in the assessment system.

Characteristic 1.2. Alternative ways to participate in assessment—other than the same way as other students, with accommodations, or in an alternate assessment—are allowed only to the extent that they are allowed for other students, and only after they have been carefully reviewed by stakeholders and policymakers, and their use and impact have been carefully studied.

Characteristic 1.3. Exemptions or exclusions from assessment are allowed for students with disabilities only to the extent that they are allowed for other students.

Principle II. Decisions about how students with disabilities participate in the assessment system are the result of clearly articulated participation, accommodations, and alternate assessment decision-making processes.

Characteristic 2.1. Decisions about how students participate in the assessment system are based on the student's ability to show what she or he knows and is able to do in the assessment formats available to all students—not on the student's instructional program, current level of functioning, or expectations about how well a student will perform.

Characteristic 2.2. Accommodations are available to all students, and decisions about use are based on student need and use in instruction.

Characteristic 2.3. The IEP team makes assessment participation, accommodation, and alternate assessment decisions on an individual student basis for each state and district assessment.

Characteristic 2.4. The IEP team documents assessment participation, accommodation, and alternate assessment decisions and the rationale for them on the IEP and reviews the decisions made for individual students and the rationale for these decisions at least annually.

Characteristic 2.5. There are clear and efficient procedures for collecting, compiling, and transferring assessment decision information from each student's IEP to state and district assessment planners and administrators.

Principle III. All students with disabilities are included when student scores are publicly reported, in the same frequency and format as all other students, whether they participate with or without accommodations, or in an alternate assessment.

Characteristic 3.1. All students in all placement settings who receive educational services are accounted for in the reporting system.

Characteristic 3.2. The number and percentage of students not in the assessment system in any way (with or without accommodations, or via an alternate assessment) are reported and an explanation given for their nonparticipation.

Characteristic 3.3. Scores that are not aggregated because of technical issues are still reported.

Characteristic 3.4. Reports are provided to educators, parents, students, policymakers, and journalists, with a clear explanation of results and implications.

(continued)

From Thurlow, Quenemoen, Thompson, and Lehr (2001).

Principle IV. The assessment performance of students with disabilities has the same impact on the final accountability index as the performance of other students, regardless of how the students participate in the assessment system (i.e., with or without accommodations, or in an alternate assessment).

Characteristic 4.1. Performance data for all students regardless of how they participate have the same impact as all other student performance data in accountability indices.

Characteristic 4.2. There are incentives for including all students in the accountability system, such as including participation rates or increase in participation rates in the accountability index.

Characteristic 4.3. There are phase-in and appeals processes for student accountability for students who have not had access to the general curriculum; but systems are held accountable immediately.

Principle V. There is improvement of the assessment system and the accountability system over time, through the processes of formal monitoring, ongoing evaluation, and systematic training in the context of emerging research and best practice.

Characteristic 5.1. All decisions about student participation, accommodations, and alternate assessment are collected, compiled, and reported, and the data are used to improve the quality of the assessment process at the school, district, and state levels.

Characteristic 5.2 The consequences of student assessment decisions are identified, compiled, and reported, and the data are reviewed by multiple stakeholders and are used to improve the quality of the accountability processes at the school, district, and state levels.

Characteristic 5.3. Based on the results of the monitoring and evaluation of the assessment and accountability systems, training is provided to multiple audiences to increase the understanding of the purpose, options, procedures, and implications of assessment options, including consequences for promotion and graduation.

Characteristic 5.4. Appropriate training for IEP teams and other key personnel is provided through collaboration of state, district, higher education (both preservice and inservice), and advocacy organizations.

Principle VI. Every policy and practice reflects the belief that *all students* must be included in state and district assessment and accountability systems

Characteristic 6.1. There is broad support in the governor's office, at the state legislature and state agencies, and among professional groups for inclusion of all students in state school reform efforts linked to assessments and accountability, demonstrated by sufficient funding and resources (e.g., staff development) designed to ensure the capacity in every school for every student to succeed.

Characteristic 6.2. All students are included in every aspect of assessment and accountability systems, including the assessments, the reporting of data, the determination of accountability measures, and the use of data for school improvement.

Characteristic 6.3. All aspects of assessment and accountability systems are designed and reviewed collaboratively, with input from other stakeholders (e.g., parents, advocacy groups, related service providers, community members), as well as general education, special education, curriculum, assessment, and administrative personnel.

FEA Principles and Primary Recommendations
from the Expert Panel on Assessment

Principle I: Equity and Capacity Building for Student Learning. Help states, districts, and schools fulfill their educational responsibilities to foster student learning and development by ensuring that all students have equitable access to the resources, tools, and information they need to succeed and by building capacity to improve teaching and learning.
1. Ensure all students have access and support to succeed in a rich curriculum. 2. Provide the equitable opportunities to learn needed to reach the ambitious goals for student achievement. 3. Focus on developing local capacity through incentives and support. 4. Match needed flexibility with increased local responsibility for implementing the law in ways that meet its goals and intents.
Principle II: Comprehensive State and Local Assessment Systems. Construct comprehensive and coherent systems of state and local assessments of student learning that work together to support instruction, educational improvement, and accountability.
1. Provide incentives for states and districts to develop comprehensive and coherent assessment systems that inform instruction and decision making in ways that state tests alone cannot and do not. Coherent and comprehensive assessment systems provide evidence of student and school performance in relation to rich and challenging educational goals, using multiple indicators of student learning from a variety of sources at multiple points in time. 2. Provide states incentives and supports to include high-quality local assessment systems in meeting ESEA's accountability requirements, alone or by augmenting state assessments. Fund pilot projects in which interested states demonstrate how they can meet ESEA's accountability requirements through standards-based, locally developed assessments of students' learning or by integrating local assessments with state assessments. Fund expansion of the number of supported projects as states indicate interest. Provide incentives for states to work together. 3. Provide tools for states and districts to self-evaluate and improve the coherence and effectiveness of their local comprehensive assessment systems. The assessment and instructional components should work together to support instructional improvement and educational accountability.
Principle III: Assessment and Accountability for Diverse Populations. Shape the design, construction, and application of assessment systems so they are appropriate for an increasingly diverse student population.
1. Design assessments based on principles of universal design but ensure that the unique factors that impact the performance of subgroups (e.g., English language learners [ELLs], students with disabilities [SWDs], students from major racial and ethnic groups, or economically disadvantaged students) are specifically addressed in the assessments that are used to measure the academic achievement of these students and reporting of results. 2. Require states to provide research-based recommendations for selecting and using appropriate accommodations for ELLs and SWDs to ensure that these students have access to valid assessments of their content knowledge. 3. Require states to validate assessment systems for each subgroup.

(continued)

4. Support research to address major issues that complicate the design of appropriate assessment systems for subgroups.

5. Provide incentives for states to work together to shape the conceptual design and construction of local and state assessments of academic achievement according to the three characteristics of each specified subgroup. Federally fund research to address the most pressing technical issues related to assessments and accountability decisions for ELLs and students with disabilities.

Principle IV: Fair Appraisal of Academic Performance. Use multiple sources of evidence to describe and interpret school and district performance fairly, based on a balance of progress toward and success in meeting student academic learning targets.

1. Encourage states and districts to use multiple sources of evidence drawn from their comprehensive and coherent systems of classroom-, school- and district-based assessments to summarize and appraise student performance.

2. Encourage states to describe school performance in terms of status, improvement, and growth, using the states' multiple sources of evidence.

3. As states evaluate their assessment systems, conduct ongoing studies of the validity of the descriptions and interpretations of student and school performance to ensure the quality of core data analysis and reporting.

Principle V: Fair Accountability Decisions. Improve the validity and reliability of criteria used to classify the performance of schools and districts to ensure fair evaluations and to minimize bias in accountability decisions.

1. Encourage states to include all subjects—not just reading, math, and science—in their comprehensive assessment systems but use compensatory processes to ensure that the inclusion of more subjects does not become another means for schools and districts to fail accountability requirements.

2. Encourage states and districts to use multiple sources of evidence drawn from their comprehensive and coherent assessment systems to make accountability decisions about the quality of school and district performance and determine which schools and districts need what forms of assistance.

3. Retain the ESEA requirement for gathering and reporting disaggregated information by subgroups based on the comprehensive assessment system.

4. Use collective research from the states to establish realistic and challenging federal guidelines for rates of growth or improvement toward the goal of reaching specified learning targets.

5. Replace the current rules for AYP classifications with reliability and validity criteria that each state must apply when designing its accountability classification system so that it is fair and minimizes bias.

6. Use accountability decisions to inform assistance to schools.

Principle VI: Use of Assessment and Accountability Information to Improve Schools and Student Learning. Provide effective, targeted assistance to schools correctly identified as needing assistance.

1. Encourage states and districts to use multiple sources of evidence drawn from their comprehensive and coherent systems of classroom-, school- and district-based assessments to summarize and appraise student performance.

2. Encourage states to describe school performance in terms of status, improvement, and growth, using the states' multiple sources of evidence.

3. As states evaluate their assessment systems, conduct ongoing studies of the validity of the descriptions and interpretations of student and school performance to ensure the quality of core data analysis and reporting.

References

Abedi, J., Courtney, C., & Leon, M. (2003). *Research supported accommodation for English Language Learners in NAEP* (CSE Tech. Rep. 586). Los Angeles: University of California, Center for Research on Evaluation, Standards, and Student Testing.

Abedi, J., Courtney, M., Leon, S., Kao, J., & Azzam, T. (2006). *English language learners and math achievement: A study of opportunity to learn and language accommodation* (CRESST Tech. Rep. No. 702). Los Angeles: University of California, National Center for Research on Evaluation, Standards, and Student Testing.

Abedi, J., Hofstetter, M., & Lord, C. (2004). Assessment accommodations for English Language Learners: Implications for policy-based empirical research. *Review of Educational Research, 74,* 1–28.

Abedi, J., Leon, S., & Mirocha, J. (2003). *Impact of student language background on content-based performance: Analyses of extant data* (CSE Tech. Rep. No. 603). Los Angeles: University of California, National Center for Research on Evaluation, Standards, and Student Testing.

Agran, M., Alper, S., & Wehmeyer, M. (2002). Access to the general education curriculum for students with significant disabilities: What it means to teacher. *Education and Training in Mental Retardation and Developmental Disabilities, 37,* 123–133.

Albus, D., Bielinski, J., Thurlow, M., & Liu, K. (2001). *The effect of a simplified English language dictionary on a reading test* (LEP Proj. Rep. 1). Minneapolis: University of Minnesota, National Center on Educational Outcomes. Retrieved December 13, 2007, from *education.umn. edu/NCEO/OnlinePubs/LEP1.html.*

Almond, P., Quenemoen, R., Olsen, K., & Thurlow, M. (2000). *Gray areas of assessment systems* (Synthesis Rep. 32). Minneapolis: University of Minnesota, National Center on Educational Outcomes.

American Educational Research Association, American Psychological Association, & National Council on Measurement in Education. (1999). *The standards for educational and psychological testing.* Washington, DC: American Educational Research Association.

American Federation of Teachers, National Council on Measurement in Education, & National Education Association. (1990). *Standards for teacher competence in educational assessment of students.* Washington, DC: Author.

Anastasi, A. (1988). *Psychological testing.* New York: Macmillan.

Anderson, L. W. (2002). Curricular alignment: A re-examination. *Theory into Practice, 41,* 255–260.

Anderson, M., Minnema, J., Thurlow, M., & Hall-Lande, J. (2005). *Confronting the unique challenges of including English language learners with disabilities in statewide assessments* (ELLs with Disabilities Rep. 9). Minneapolis: University of Minnesota, National Center on Educational Outcomes.

Avramidis, E., & Norwich, B. (2002). Teachers' attitudes toward integration/inclusion: A review of the literature. *European Journal of Special Needs Education, 17,* 129–147.

Baker, E. L., Bewley, W. L., Herman, J. L., Lee, J. J., & Mitchell, D. S. (2001). *Upgrading America's use of information to improve student perjormance* (Proposal to the U.S. Secretary of Education). Los Angeles: University of California, National Center for Research on Evaluation, Standards, and Student Testing.

Baker, E. L., & Linn, R. I. (2002). *Validity issues for accountability systems.* Los Angeles: University of California, National Center for Research on Evaluation, Standards, and Student Testing.

Baxter, J., Woodward, J., Voorhies, J., & Wong, J. (2002). We talk about it, but do they get it? *Learning Disabilities Research and Practice, 17*(3), 173–185.

Bennett, R. E., Rock, D. A., & Kaplan, B. A. (1987). SAT differential item performance for nine handicapped groups. *Journal of Educational Measurement, 24*(1), 41–55.

Bennett, R. E., Rock, D. A., & Novatkoski, I. (1989). Differential item functioning on the SAT-M Braille edition. *Journal of Educational Measurement, 26*(1), 67–79.

Berry, J. W., Poortinga, Y. H., Segall, M. H., & Dasen, P. R. (2002). *Cross-cultural psychology: Research and applications* (2nd ed.). Cambridge, UK: Cambridge University Press.

Blanding, K. M., Richards, J., Bradley-Johnson, S., & Johnson, C. M. (1994). The effect of token reinforcement on McCarthy Scale Performance for white preschoolers of low and high social position. *Journal of Behavioral Education, 4,* 33–39.

Bolt, S., & Decker, D. (2007, March). *The alignment of accommodations provided across high school and college.* Paper presented at the annual meeting of the National Association of School Psychologists, New York.

Bolt, S. E., & Thurlow, M. L. (2004). Five of the most commonly allowed accommodations in state policy: Synthesis of research. *Remedial and Special Education, 25,* 141–152.

Bolt, S. E., & Thurlow, M. L. (2007). Item-level effects of the read-aloud accommodation for students with reading disabilities. *Assessment for Effective Intervention, 31,* 15–28.

Bolt, S. E., & Ysseldyke, J. E. (2008). Accommodating students with disabilities in large-scale testing: A comparison of differential item functioning (DIF) identified across disability types. *Journal of Psychoeducational Assessment, 26,* 121–138.

Bottsford-Miller, N., Thurlow, M. L., Stout, K. E., & Quenemoen, R. F. (2006). *A comparison of IEP/504 accommodations under classroom and standardized testing conditions: A preliminary report on SEELS Data* (Synthesis Rep. 63). Minneapolis: University of Minnesota, National Center on Educational Outcomes. Retrieved May 27, 2008, from *education.umn.edu/NCEO/OnlinePubs/Synthesis63.*

Bridgeman, B., Harvey, A., & Braswell, J. (1995). Effects of calculator use on scores on a test of mathematical reasoning. *Journal of Educational Measurement, 32*(4), 323–340.

Brophy, J. (1983). Research on the self-fulfilling prophecy and teacher expectations. *Journal of Educational Psychology, 75,* 631–661.

Browder, D. M., & Cooper-Duffy, K. (2003). Evidence-based practices for students with severe disabilities and the requirements for accountability in "No Child Left Behind." *Journal of Special Education, 37,* 157–165.

Browder, D. M., Fallin, K., Davis, S., & Karvonen, M. (2003). Consideration of what may influence student outcomes on alternate assessment. *Education and Training in Developmental Disabilities, 38,* 255–270.

Browder, D. M., Flowers, C., Ahlgrim-Delzell, L., Karvonen, M., Spooner, F., & Algozzine, R. (2004). The alignment of alternate assessment content to academic and functional curricula. *Journal of Special Education, 37,* 211–224.

Browder, D. M., Spooner, F., Algozzine, R., Ahlgrim-Delzell, L., Flowers, C., & Karvonen, M. (2003). What we know and need to know about alternate assessment. *Exceptional Children, 70,* 45–61.

Browder, D. M., Wakeman, S. Y., Flowers, C., Rickelman, R., Pugalee. D., & Karvonen, M. (2007). Creating access to the general curriculum with links to grade level content for students with significant cognitive disabilities: An explication of the concept. *Journal of Special Education, 41,* 2–16.

Browder, D. M., Wakeman, S. Y., Spooner, F., Ahlgrim-Delzell, L., & Algozzine, B. (2006). Research on reading instruction for individuals with significant cognitive disabilities. *Exceptional Children, 72,* 392–408.

Browder, D. M., & Xin, Y. (1998). A review and meta-analysis of sight word instruction with students with disabilities. *Journal of Special Education, 32,* 130–153.

Brown, P. J. (1998). *Findings of the 1997 spring field test.* Retrieved September 4, 2002, from *www.doe. state.de.us/aab/dstp%SFresearch.html.*

Burk, M. (1999). *Computerized test accommodations.* Washington, DC: A. U. Software.

Burns, E. (1998). *Test accommodations for students with disabilities.* Springfield, IL: Charles C Thomas.

Capper, C. A., Frattura, E., & Keyes, M. W. (2000). *Meeting the needs of students of all abilities: How leaders go beyond inclusion.* Thousand Oaks, CA: Corwin Press.

Capps, R., Fix, M., Murray, J., Ost, J., Passel, J., & Hernandez, S. (2005). *The new demography of American schools: Immigration and the No Child Left Behind Act.* Washington, DC: Urban Institute. Retrieved November 19, 2007, from *www.urban.org/UploadedPDF/311230_new_demography.pdf.*

Cazden, C. (1988). *Classroom discourse: The language of teaching and learning.* Portsmouth, NH: Heinemann.

Center for Universal Design. (1997). *The Principles of Universal Design, Version 2.0.* Raleigh, NC: North Carolina State University.

Chiu, C. W. T., & Pearson, P. D. (1999, June). *Synthesizing the effects of test accommodations for special education and limited English proficiency students.* Paper presented at the National Conference on Large Scale Assessment, Snowbird, UT (ERIC Document Reproduction Service No. ED 433 362)

Clapper, A. T., Morse, A. B., Thompson, S. J., & Thurlow, M. L. (2005). *Access assistants for state assessments: A study of state guidelines for scribes, readers, and sign language interpreters* (Synthesis Rep. 58). Minneapolis: University of Minnesota, National Center on Educational Outcomes. Retrieved December 26, 2006, from *education.umn.edu/NCEO/OnlinePubs/Synthesis58.html.*

Cohen, A. S., & Kim, S. (1992). Detecting calculator effects on item performance. *Applied Measurement in Education, 5*(4), 303–320.

Collier, V. P. (1987). Age and rate of acquisition of second language for academic purposes. *TESOL Quarterly, 21,* 617–641.

Cortiella, C. (2007). *Learning opportunities for your child through alternate assessments: Alternate assessments based on modified academic achievement standards.* Minneapolis: University of Minnesota, National Center on Educational Outcomes. Available at *www.nceo.info/OnlinePubs/ AAMAAParentGuide.pdf.*

Council of Chief State School Officers. (2002). *Trainer of trainers materials on the assessment of ELL students.* Retrieved June 27, 2007, from *www.ccsso.org/content.pdfs/EllTrainerOfTrainersSlides.pdf.*

Council of Chief State School Officers. (2003). *Glossary of assessment terms and acronyms.* Washington, DC: Authors.

Cummins, J. (1984). *Bilingualism and special education: Issues in assessment and pedagogy.* Clevedon, UK: Multilingual Matters.

Diaz-Rico, L. T., & Weed, K. Z. (2002). *The crosscultural language and academic development handbook: A complete reference guide* (2nd ed.). Boston: Allyn-Bacon.

Dolan, B. (2000). Universal design for learning: Associate editor's column. *Journal of Special Education Technology, 15,* 47–51.

Dolan, R. P., Hall, T. E., Banerjee, M., Chun, E., & Strangman, N. (2005). Applying principles of universal design to test delivery: The effect of computer-based read-aloud on test performance of high school students with learning disabilities. *Journal of Technology, Learning, and Assessment, 3*(7). Available at *www.jtla.org.*

Duncan, T., Parent, L., Chen, W., Ferrara, S., Johnson, E., Oppler, S., & Shieh, Y. (2005). Study of a dual-language test booklet in eighth-grade mathematics. *Applied Measurement in Education, 18*(2), 129–161.

Duran, R. P., Brown, C., & McCall, M. (2002). Assessment of English language learners in the Oregon statewide assessment system: National and state perspectives. In G. Tindal & T. Haladyna (Eds.), *Large scale assessment programs for all students* (pp. 371–394). Mahwah, NJ: Erlbaum.

Elliott, S. N. (2001). *Enhancing the Wisconsin Alternate Assessment project proposal.* Madison: Wisconsin Department of Public Instruction.

Elliott, S. N. (2006, October). *Using the Mississippi Alternate Assessment wuth students with the most significant disabilities.* Jackson: Mississippi Department of Education.

Elliott, S. N., Braden, J., & White, J. (2001). *Assessing one and all: Educational accountability for students with disabilities.* Arlington, VA: Council for Exceptional Children.

Elliott, S. N., & Fuchs, L. S. (1997). The utility of CBM and performance assessment as alternatives to traditional intelligence tests. *School Psychology Review, 26,* 224–233.

Elliott, S. N., Kratochwill, T. R., & McKevitt, B. C. (2001). Experimental analysis of the effects of testing accommodations on the scores of students with and without disabilities. *Journal of School Psychology, 39*(1), 3–24.

Elliott, S. N., & Roach, A. T. (2007). Alternate assessments of students with significant disabilities: Alternative approaches, common technical challenges. *Applied Measurement in Education, 20,* 301–333.

Elmore, R. (2003). *Knowing the right thing to do: Low-performing schools and pelformance-based accountability.* Washington, DC: National Governors Association, Center for Best Practices.

Elmore, R. F., Abelman, C. H., & Fuhrman, S. H. (1996). The new accountability in state education reform: From process to performance. In H. F. Ladd (Ed.), *Holding schools accountable: Performance-based reform in education* (pp. 65–98). Washington, DC: Brookings Institute.

Essex, N. L. (2006). *What every teacher should know about No Child Left Behind.* Boston: Pearson Education.

Fisher, D., & Frey, N. (2001). Access to the core curriculum: Critical ingredients for student success. *Remedial and Special Education, 22,* 148–157.

Flowers, C., Wakeman, S. Y., Browder, D., & Karvonen, M.(2007). *Links for academic learning: An alignment protocol for alternate assessments based on alternate achievement standards.* Charlotte: National Alternate Assessment Center, University of North Carolina at Charlotte.

Ford, A., Davern, L., & Schnorr, R. (2001). Learners with significant disabilities: Curricular relevance in an era of standards-based reform. *Remedial and Special Education, 22,* 214–222.

Forum on Educational Accountability. (2007). *Assessment and accountability for improving schools and learning: Principles and recommendations for federal law and state and local systems.* Available at *www.edaccountability.org.*

Francis, D., Rivera, M., Lesaux, N., Kieffer, M., & Rivera, H. (2006). *Practical guidelines for the education of English Language Learners: Research-based recommendations for the use of accommodations in large-scale assessments.* Portsmouth, NH: Center on Instruction at RMC Research Corporation. Retrieved June 27, 2007, from *www.centeroninstruction.org/files/ELL3–Assessments.pdf.*

Fuchs, L., Fuchs, D., & Capizzi, A. (2005). Identifying appropriate accommodations for students with learning disabilities. *Focus on Exceptional Children, 37,* 1–9.

Fuchs, L., Fuchs, D., Eaton, S., & Hamlett, C. (2002). *Dynamic assessment of test accommodations.* San Antonio, TX: Psychological Corporation.

Fuchs, L. S., Fuchs, D., Eaton, S., & Hamlett, C. (2003). *Dynamic assessment of test accommodations.* San Antonio, TX: Harcourt Assessment.

Fuchs, L. S., Fuchs, D., Eaton, S. B., Hamlett, C., Binkley, E., & Crouch, R. (2000). Using objective data source to enhance teacher judgments about test accommodations. *Exceptional Children, 67,* 67–81.

Fuchs, L. S., Fuchs, D., Eaton, S. B., Hamlett, C. L., & Karns, K. M. (2000). Supplementing teacher judgments of mathematics test accommodations with objective data sources. *School Psychology Review, 29,* 65–85.

Fullan, M. (1996). Turning systemic thinking on its head. *Phi Delta Kappa, 77*(6), 420–425.

Fullan, M. (2003). *Change forces with a vengeance.* New York: Rutledge Falmer.

Gajria, M., Salend, S. J., & Hemrick, M. A. (1994). Teacher acceptability of testing modifications for mainstreamed students. *Learning Disabilities Research and Practice, 9*(4), 236–243.

Glatthorn, A. A., Bragaw, D., Dawkins, K., & Parker, J. (1998). *Performance assessment and standards-based curricula: The achievement cycle.* Larchmont, NY: Eye on Education.

Graham, S., & Harris, K. R. (2003). Students with learning disabilities and the process of writing: A meta-analysis of SRSD studies. In L. H. Swanson, K. R. Harris, & S. Graham (Eds)., *Handbook of learning disabilities* (pp. 323–344). New York: Guilford Press.

Haladyna, T. M. (2002). Research to improve large-scale testing. In G. Tindal and T. M. Haladyna's Large-scale assessment programs for all students: Validity, technical adequacy, and implementation. In G. Tindal & T. Haladyna (Eds.), *Large scale assessment programs for all students* (pp. 483–497). Mahwah, NJ: Erlbaum.

Hambleton, R. K., & Patsula, L. (1998). Adapting tests for use in multiple languages and cultures. *Social Indicators Research, 45,* 153–171.

Harbin, G., Rous, B., & McLean, M. (2005). Issues in designing statewide systems of accountability. *Journal of Early Intervention, 27*(3), 137–164.

Hehir, T. (2005). *New directions in special education: Eliminating ableism in policy and practice.* Cambridge, MA: Harvard University Press.

Herman, J. L., Klein, D., & Abedi, J. (2000). Assessing students' opportunity to learn: Teacher and student perspectives. *Educational Measurement: Issues and Practice, 19,* 16–24.

Hitchcock, C., Meyer, A., Rose, D., & Jackson, R. (2002). Providing new access to the general curriculum: Universal Design for Learning. *Teaching Exceptional Children, 35*(2), 8–17.

Hoge, R. D., & Coladarci, T. (1989). Teacher-based judgments of academic achievement: A review of the literature. *Review of Educational Research, 59,* 297–313.

Hollenbeck, K. (2002). Determining when test alterations are valid accommodations or modifications for large-scale assessment. In G. Tindal & T. Haladyna (Eds.), *Large scale assessment programs for all students* (pp. 395–425). Mahwah, NJ: Erlbaum.

Hollenbeck, K., Rozek-Tedesco, M. A., Tindal, G., & Glasgow A. (2000). An exploratory study of student-paced versus teacher-paced accommodations for large-scale math tests. *Journal of Special Education Technology, 15*(2), 27–36.

Individuals with Disabilities Education Act Amendments of 1997, Public Law 105-17, 111 Stat. 37 (codified as amended at 20 U. S. C. § 1400 *et seq.*).

Individuals with Disabilities Education Improvement Act of 2004, 20 U. S. C.

Jayanthi, M., Epstein, M. H., Polloway, E. A., & Bursuck, W. D. (1996). A national survey of general education teachers' perceptions of testing adaptations. *Journal of Special Education, 30*(1), 99–115.

Johnstone, C. J., Altman, J., & Thurlow, M. (2006). *A state guide to the development of universally designed assessments.* Minneapolis: University of Minnesota, National Center on Educational Outcomes.

Johnstone, C. J., Altman, J., Thurlow, M. L., & Thompson, S. J. (2006). *A summary of research on the effects of test accommodations: 2002 through 2004* (Technical Report 45). Minneapolis: University of Minnesota, National Center on Educational Outcomes. Retrieved May 17, 2008, from *education. umn.edu/NCEO/OnlinePubs/Tech45.*

Johnstone, C. J., Thompson, S. J., Moen, R. E., Bolt, S., & Kato, K. (2005). *Analyzing results of large-scale assessments to ensure universal design* (Tech. Rep. 41). Minneapolis: University of Minnesota, National Center on Educational Outcomes. Retrieved December 13, 2007, from *education.umn. edu/NCEO/OnlinePubs/Technical41.htm.*

Kampfer, S. H., Horvath, L. S., Kleinert, H. L., & Kearns, J. F. (2001). Teachers' perceptions of one state's alternate assessment: Implications for practice and preparation. *Exceptional Children, 67,* 361–374.

Karger, J. (2004). *Access to the general curriculum for students with disabilities: the role of the IEP.* Wakefield, MA: National Center on Accessing the General Curriculum. Retrieved May 17, 2008, from *www.cast.org/publications/ncac/ncac_iep.html.*

King-Sears, M. E. (2001). Three steps for gaining access to the general curriculum for learners with disabilities. *Intervention in School and Clinic, 37,* 67–76.

Kleinert, H., Green, P., Hurte, M., Clayton, G., & Oetinger, C. (2002). Creating and using meaningful alternate assessments. *Teaching Exceptional Children, 34,* 40–47.

Kleinert, H. L., Kennedy, S., & Kearns, J. F. (1999). The impact of alternate assessments: A statewide teacher survey. *Journal on Special Education, 33,* 93–102

Koegel, L. K., Koegel, R. L., & Smith, A. (1997). Variables related to differences in standardized test outcomes for children with autism. *Journal of Autism and Developmental Disorders, 27,* 233–243.

Koertz, D., McCaffrey, D., Klein, S., Bell, R., & Stecher, B. (1993). *The reliability of scores from the 1992 Vermont portfolio assessment program* (CSE Tech. Rep. 355). Los Angeles: National Center for Research on Evaluation, Standards, and Student Testing.

Kopriva, R. (2000). *Ensuring accuracy in testing for English language learners.* Washington, DC: Council of Chief State School Officers.

Kopriva, R., Emick, J., Hipolito-Delgado, C., & Cameron, C. (2007). Do proper accommodation assignments make a difference?: Examining the impact of improved decision-making on scores for English Language Learners. *Educational Measurement: Issues and Practice, 26,* 11–20.

Koretz, D. M. (1997). *The assessment of students with disabilities in Kentucky* (CSE Technical Report No. 431). Los Angeles: University of California, Los Angeles, Center for Research on Evaluation, Standards, and Student Testing.

Koretz, D. M., & Barton, K. (2003). *Assessing students with disabilities: Issues and evidence* (CSE Technical Rep. 587). Los Angeles: University of California, Center for the Study of Evaluation Retrieved from *cse.ucla.edu/reports/TR587.pdf.*

Kosciolek, S., & Ysseldyke, J. E. (2000). *Effects of a reading accommodation on the validity of a reading test* (Tech. Rep. 28). Minneapolis: University of Minnesota, National Center on Educational Outcomes.

Lewis, S. (1996). The reading achievements of a group of severely and profoundly hearing-impaired school leavers educated within a natural aural approach. *Journal of British Association of Teachers of the Deaf, 20*(1), 1–7.

Lewis, D. M., Mitzel, H. C., & Green, D. R. (1996, June). Standard setting: A bookmark approach. In D. R. Green (Chair), *IRT-based standard-setting procedures utilizing behavioral anchoring.* Symposium conducted at the meeting of the Council of Chief State School Officers National Conference on Large Scale Assessment, Phoenix, AZ.

Lipsky, D., & Gartner, A. (1996). Inclusion, school restructuring and the remaking of American society. *Harvard Educational Review, 66*(4), 762–796.

Loyd, B. H. (1991). Mathematics test performance: The effects of item type and calculator use. *Applied Measurement in Education, 4*(1), 11–22.

Mason, C., Field, S., & Sawilosky, S. (2004). Implementation of self-determination activities and student participation in IEPs. *Exceptional Children, 70,* 441–451.

McKevitt, B. C., & Elliott, S. N. (2003). Effects and perceived consequences of using read-aloud and teacher-recommended testing accommodations on a reading achievement test. *School Psychology Review, 32*(4), 583–600.

Mehan, H. (1979). *Learning lessons.* Cambridge, MA: Harvard University Press.

Meloy, L. L., Deville, C., & Frisbie, D. A. (2002). The effect of a read-aloud accommodation on test scores of students with and without a learning disability in reading. *Remedial and Special Education, 23*(4), 248–255.

Mondale, S., & Patton, S. B. (2002). *School: The story of American public education.* Boston: Beacon Press.

Morocco, K. C. (2001). Teaching for understanding with students with disabilities: New directions for research on access to the general education curriculum. *Learning Disability Quarterly, 24,* 5–13.

National Center for Education Statistics. (2004). *Language minority learners and their labor market indicators—Recent trends. NCES 2004–009.* Washington, DC: Department of Education. Retrieved June 27, 2007, from *nces.ed.gov/pubs2004/2004009.pdf.*

Nietupski, J., Harme-Nietupski, S., Curtin, S., & Shrikanth, K. (1997). A review of curricular research in severe disabilities from 1976–1995 in six selected journals. *Journal of Special Education, 31,* 36–55.

Nolet, V., & McLaughlin, M. J. (2000). Accessing the general curriculum: Including students with disabilities in standards-based reform. Thousand Oaks, CA: Corwin Press.

O'Brien, J., & O'Brien, C. L. (1995). *Inclusion as a force for school renewal.* Syracuse, NY: Center on Human Policy.

O'Day, J. A. (2002). Complexity, accountability, and school improvement. *Harvard Educational Review, 72*(3), 293–329.

Olson, J. F., & Goldstein, A. A. (1996). Increasing the inclusion of students with disabilities and limited English proficient students in NAEP. *Focus on NAEP, 2*(1). Washington, DC: National Center for Education Statistics.

Organization for Economic Cooperation and Development. (2000). *Knowledge and skills for life: First results from PISA 2000.* Paris: Author.

Phillips, S. E. (2002). Legal issues affecting special populations in large-scale testing programs. In G. Tindal & T. Haladyna (Eds.), *Large scale assessment programs for all students* (pp. 109–148). Mahwah, NJ: Erlbaum.

Pisha, B., & Coyne, P. (2001). Smart from the start: The promise of universal design for learning. *Remedial and Special Education, 22,* 197–203.

Pugach, M. C., & Warger, C. L. (2001). Curriculum matters: Raising expectations for students with disabilities. *Remedial and Special Education, 22,* 194–196.

Quenemoen, R., Thompson, S., Thurlow, M., & Lehr, C. (2001). *A self-study guide to implementation of inclusive assessment and accountability systems: A best practice approach.* Minneapolis, MN: National Center on Educational Outcomes. Retrieved May 17, 2008, from: cehd.umn.edu/NCEO/OnlinePubs/workbook.pdf.

Ravitch, D. (1995). *National standards in American education: A citizen's guide.* Washington, DC: Brookings Institution.

Redfield, R., Linton, R., & Herskovis, M. J. (1936). Memorandum for the study of acculturation. *American Anthropologist, 38,* 149–152.

Resnick, L. B., Rothman, R., Slattery, J. B., & Vranek, J. L. (2003). Benchmarking and alignment of standards and testing. *Educational Assessment, 9,* 1–27.

Ritzer, G. (2000). *The McDonaldization of society: New century edition.* Thousand Oaks, CA: Pine Forge Press.

Roach, A. T. (2005). Alternate assessment as the "ultimate accommodation": Four challenges for policy and practice. *Assessment for Effective Intervention, 31,* 73–78.

Roach, A. T., & Elliott, S. N. (2004, April). *Alignment analysis and standard setting procedures for alternate assessments.* Paper presented at the annual meeting of the American Educational Research Association, San Diego, CA.

Roach, A. T., & Elliott, S. N. (2006). Influence of access to the general education curriculum on the alternate assessment performance of students with significant cognitive disabilities. *Educational Evaluation and Policy Analysis, 28,* 181–194.

Roach, A. T., & Elliott, S. N. (in press). Consultation to support inclusive accountability and standards-based reform: Facilitating access, equity, and empowerment. *Journal of Educational and Psychological Consultation.*

Roach, A. T., Elliott, S. N., & Berndt. S. A. (2007). Teacher satisfaction and the consequential validity of an alternate assessment for students with significant cognitive disabilities. *Journal of Disability Policy Studies, 18,* 168–175.

Roach, A. T., Elliott, S. N., & Webb. N. L. (2005). Alignment of an alternate assessment with state academic standards: Evidence for the content validity of the Wisconsin Alternate Assessment. *Journal of Special Education, 38*, 218–231.

Roach, A. T., & Frank, J. L. (2007). Large-scale assessment, rationality, and scientific management: The case of No Child Left Behind. *Journal of Applied School Psychology, 23*, 7–25.

Roach, A. T., McGrath, D. C., & Wixson, C. S. (2008). *Alignment of the Indiana Standards Tool for Alternate Reporting to state kindergarten standards: Extending a nationally recognized alignment framework for use with early childhood accountability systems.* Manuscript submitted for publication.

Roach, A. T., McGrath, D. C., & Wixson, C. S. (2008). *Extending a nationally recognized alignment framework for use with early childhood accountability systems.* Unpublished manuscript.

Roach, A. T., Niebling, B. C., & Kurz, A. (2008). Evaluating the alignment among curriculum, instruction, and assessment: Implications and applications for research and practice. *Psychology in the Schools, 45*, 158–176.

Rogers, W. T. (1983). Use of separate answer sheets with hearing impaired and deaf school age students. *B. C. Journal of Special Education, 7*(1), 63–72.

Rose, D. (2001). Universal design for learning: Deriving guiding principles from networks that learn. *Journal of Special Education Technology, 16*, 66–67.

Rose, D., & Meyer, A. (2006). *A practical reader in Universal design for learning* Cambridge, MA: Harvard Education Press.

Salvia, J., Ysseldyke, J., & Bolt, S. (2007). *Assessment in special and inclusive education* (10th ed.). New York: Houghton-Mifflin.

Scheurich, J. J., Skrla, L., & Johnson, J. F. (2004). Thinking carefully about accountability and equity. In L. Skrla & J. J. Scheurich (Eds.), *Educational equity and accountability: Policies, paradigms, and politics* (pp. 13–27). New York: Routledge Falmer.

Schulte, A. G., Elliott, S. N., & Kratochwill, T. R. (2001). Experimental analysis of the effects of testing accommodations on students' standardized achievement test scores. *School Psychology Review, 30*(4), 527–547.

Shriner, J., & DeStefano, L. (2003). Participation and accommodation in state assessment: The role of individualized education programs. *Exceptional Children, 69*, 147–161.

Simmons, D. C., & Kame'enui, E. J. (1996). A focus on curriculum design: When children fail. *Focus on Exceptional Children, 28*(7), 1–22.

Sireci, S. G. (1997). Problems and issues in linking assessments across languages *Educational Measurement: Issues and Practice, 16*(1), 12–19.

Sireci, S. G., & Khaliq, S. N. (2002). *An analysis of the psychometric properties of dual language test forms* (Center for Educational Assessment Res. Rep. No. 458). Amherst: University of Massachusetts, School of Education.

Sireci, S., Yang, Y., Harter, J., & Ehrlich, E. (2006). Evaluating guidelines for test adaptations: A methodological analysis of translation quality. *Journal of Cross-Cultural Psychology, 37*, 557–567.

Snyder, P. A., Wixson, C., Talapatra, D., & Roach, A. T. (in press). Assessment in early intervention and early childhood special education: Developing and validating intervention- and instruction-focused strategies. *Assessment for Effective Intervention.*

Spillane, J. P. (1999). External reform initiatives and teachers' efforts to reconstruct their practice: The mediating role of teachers' zones of enactment. *Journal of Curriculum Studies, 31*, 143–175.

Spillane, J. P., Reiser, B. J., & Reimer, T. (2002). Policy implementation and cognition: Reframing and refocusing implementation research. *Review of Educational Research, 72*, 387–431.

Spooner, F., & Browder, D. (2006). Why teach the general curriculum? In D. Browder & F. Spooner (Eds.), *Teaching language arts, math, and science to students with cognitive disabilities.* Baltimore: Brookes.

Stiggins, R. J. (1999). Evaluating classroom assessment training in teacher education programs. *Educational Measurement: Issues and Practice, 18*, 23–27.

Test, D., Fowler, C., Wood, W., Brewer, B., & Eddy, S. (2005). A conceptual framework of self-advocacy for students with disabilities. *Remedial and Special Education, 26,* 43–54.

Thompson, S. J., Johnstone, C. J., & Thurlow, M. L. (2002). *Universal design applied to large scale assessments* (Synthesis Report 44). Minneapolis: University of Minnesota, National Center on Educational Outcomes. Retrieved December 13, 2007, from *education.umn.edu/NCEO/OnlinePubs/Synthesis44.html.*

Thompson, S. J., Johnstone, C. J., Thurlow, M. L., & Altman, J. R. (2005). *2005 State special education outcomes: Steps forward in a decade of change.* Minneapolis: University of Minnesota, National Center on Educational Outcomes. Retrieved December 26, 2006, from *education.umn.edu/NCEO/OnlinePubs/2005StateReport.htm.*

Thompson, S., Morse, A., Sharpe, M., & Hall, S. (2005). *Accommodations manual: How to select, administer, and evaluate use of accommodations for instruction and assessment of students with disabilities* (2nd ed.). Washington, DC: Council of Chief State School Officers.

Thompson, S., Quenemoen, R., Thurlow, M., & Ysseldyke, J. (2001). *Alternate assessments for students with disabilities.* Thousand Oaks, CA: Corwin Press.

Thompson, S., Thurlow, M., Quenemoen, R., Esler, A., & Whetstone, P. (2001). *Addressing standards and assessments on the IEP* (Synthesis Rep. 38). Minneapolis: University of Minnesota, National Center on Educational Outcomes. Retrieved December 26, 2006, from *education.umn.edu/NCEO/OnlinePubs/Synthesis38.html.*

Thurlow, M., Albus, D., Shyyan, V., Liu, K., & Barrera, M. (2004). *Educator perceptions of instructional strategies for standards-based education of English language learners with disabilities* (ELLs with Disabilities Rep. 7). Minneapolis: University of Minnesota, National Center on Educational Outcomes.

Thurlow, M., Elliott, J., & Ysseldyke, J. (2003). *Testing students with disabilities: Practical strategies for complying with district and state requirements* (2nd ed.). Thousand Oaks, CA: Corwin Press.

Thurlow, M., Olsen, K., Elliott, J., Ysseldyke, J., Erickson, R., & Ahern, E. (1996). Alternate assessments for students with disabilities. *NCEO Policy Directions, 5,* 1–6.

Thurlow, M., Quenemoen, R., Thompson, S., & Lehr, C. (2001). *Principles and characteristics of inclusive assessment and accountability systems* (Synthesis Rep. 40). Minneapolis: University of Minnesota, National Center on Educational Outcomes. Retrieved from August 1, 2008, from *education.umn.edu/NCEO/OnlinePubs/Synthesis40.html.*

Thurlow, M. L., Ysseldyke, J. E., & Silverstein, B. (1993). *Testing accommodations for students with disabilities: A review of the literature* (Synthesis Rep. 4). Minneapolis: National Center on Educational Outcomes.

Tindal, G., Heath, B., Hollenbeck, K., Almond, P., & Harniss, M. (1998). Accommodating students with disabilities on large-scale tests: An experimental study. *Exceptional Children, 64*(4), 439–450.

Tindal, G., McDonald, M., Tedesco, M., Glasgow, A., Almond, P., Crawford, L., & Hollenbeck, K. (2003). Alternate assessments in reading and math: Development and validation for students with significant disabilities. *Exceptional Children, 69,* 481–494.

Tolfa-Veit, D., & Scruggs,T. E. (1986). Can learning disabled students effectively use separate answer sheets? *Perceptual and Motor Skills, 63,* 155–160.

Trimble, S. (1998). *Performance trends and use of accommodations on a statewide assessment* (Maryland–Kentucky Rep. No. 3). Minneapolis: University of Minnesota, National Center on Educational Outcomes.

Turner, M. D., Baldwin, L., Kleinert, H. L., & Kearns, J. F. (2000). The relation of a statewide alternate assessment for students with severe disabilities to other measures of instructional effectiveness. *Journal of Special Education, 34,* 69–76.

United States Department of Education. (1994). *Goals 2000: Reforming education to improve student achievement.* Washington, DC: Author.

United States Department of Education. (2003, December). *Final regulations for the inclusion of students with the most significant cognitive disabilities in Title 1 assessments.* Washington, DC: Author.

United States Department of Education. (2003). *Report cards: Title I, Part A Non-Regulatory Guidance.* Washington, DC: Author.

United States Department of Education. (2005, August). *Alternate achievement standards for students with the most significant cognitive disabilities: Non-regulatory guidance.* Washington, DC: Author.

United States Department of Education. (2007, July). *Modified academic achievement standards: Non-regulatory guidance.* Washington, DC: Author.

Warlick, K., & Towles-Reeves, L. (2005, July). *National Alternate Assessment Center overview.* Washington, DC: OSEP Project Directors' Conference.

Webb, N. L. (1997). *Criteria for alignment of expectations and assessments in mathematics and science education* (NISE Res. Monog. No. 6). Madison: University of Wisconsin–Madison, National Institute for Science Education.

Webb, N. L. (2002, April). *An analysis of the alignment between mathematics standards and assessments for three states.* Paper presented at the annual meeting of the American Educational Research Association, New Orleans, LA.

Wehmeyer, M. L. (2003). Defining mental retardation and ensuring access to the general curriculum. *Education and Training in Developmental Disabilities, 38,* 271–282.

Wehmeyer, M. L., Lance, G. D., & Bashinski, S. (2002). Promoting access to the general curriculum for students with mental retardation: A multi-level model. *Education and Training in Mental Retardation and Developmental Disabilities, 37,* 223–234.

Weston, T. J. (1999). Investigating the validity of the accommodation of oral presentation in testing (doctoral dissertation, University of Colorado, 1999). *Dissertation Abstracts International, 60,* A1083.

Weston, T. J. (1999, April). *The validity of oral presentation in testing.* Paper presented at the annual meeting of the American Educational Research Association, Seattle, WA.

Wiener, D. (2006). *Alternate assessments measured against grade-level achievement standards: The Massachusetts "Competency Portfolio"* (Synthesis Rep. 59). Minneapolis: University of Minnesota, National Center on Educational Outcomes. Retrieved May 17, 2008, from *education.umn.edu/NCEO/OnlinePubs/Synthesis59.html.*

Willis, J., & Shibata, B. (1978). A comparison of tangible reinforcement and feedback effects on the WPPSI I. Q. scores of nursery school children. *Education and Treatment of Children, 1,* 31–45.

Wise, A. (1996). Building a system of quality assurance for the teaching profession: Moving into the 21st century. *Phi Delta Kappan, 78,* 191–192.

Wolf, M. K., Kao, J., Herman, J., Bachman, L. F., Bailey, A., Bachman, P. L., et al. (2008). *Issues in assessing English language learners: English language proficiency measures and accommodation uses—literature review* (CRESST Rep. 731). Los Angeles: Center for Research on Evaluation, Standards, and Student Testing.

Yell, M. L. (1998). *The law and special education.* Upper Saddle River, NJ: Merrill.

Ysseldyke, J., Thurlow, M., McGrew, K., & Shriner, J. (1994). *Recommendations for making decisions about the participation of students with disabilities in statewide assessment programs* (Synthesis Rep. 15). Minneapolis: University of Minnesota, National Center on Educational Outcomes.

Ysseldyke, J., Thurlow, M., McGrew, K., & Vanderwood, M. (1994). *Making decisions about the inclusion of students with disabilities in large-scale assessments* (Synthesis Rep. 13). Minneapolis: National Center on Educational Outcomes.

Ysseldyke, J., Thurlow, M., & Shin, H. (1995). *Opportunity-to-learn standards* (Policy Directions No. 4). Minneapolis: National Center on Educational Outcomes. Retrieved May 17, 2008, from *education.umn.edu/NCEO/OnlinePubs/Policy4.html.*

Index

Page numbers in italics indicate figures or tables.